WHISPER MARKETING

"The Secret Restaurant Formula"

Ronald "Bo" Bryant

Book 1 in the "7P" series

Visit BoBryant.com

ISBN-13: 978-1494466961
ISBN-10: 1494466961

DEDICATION

To Emily and Asher, my beautiful, crazy children who keep me creative and young. And of course to my wife, for having the patience of a saint and the belief that I will change the world!

CONTENTS

ACKNOWLEDGMENTS

I would like to acknowledge and thank all of the amazing people in this business I have been so fortunate to work with.

The chefs that trained me and took me under their collective wings. The guys who taught me the true beauty of food and the importance of technique and yet still encouraged me to challenge everything about food.

To Goose Sorenson and Paul Gummerson who inspired me with amazing stories of how to fight with your back up against the wall and always be the last man standing. For letting me ask the stupid questions and growing with me. And to Tyler Wiard, for forcing me to be better!

My father for trying to teach me humility and grace and to challenge everything.
My mother for believing in me blindly to the point that I discovered I was not capable of failure.

My father who tried to teach me humility and grace. And to challenge the legacy thinking. The world won't be the same without you.

To those who told me I would fail! I thank you more than anyone else! Without giving me someone to prove wrong, I would have never succeeded at anything.

To the innovators, the little guys, the believers, the passionate and the underdogs, I tip my hat to you. You inspire me every day!

To the "crazy" authors like Godin and Gladwell for teaching me it was okay to be different and more importantly to run with it.

And most importantly, to those who take risks and make shit happen!

INTRODUCTION

"If you give a boy a hammer, the world is his nail."
~ My father

If you are in the restaurant business, you are either the guy who is killing it or the guy getting killed. Why do some restaurants open their doors with seemingly no effort and become an overnight success while others fight tooth and nail every day barely getting by? The answer is simple. There is a secret formula that is barely audible throughout the industry. A mere "Whisper" that gets the crowd's attention. A viral equation that makes a concept work. And if you listen closely, you will hear it... If you pay attention, you can create it!

Quit focusing on the why? Pay attention to the what, the how, the where and the when.

I have had the pleasure of working in this secret circle for years. To hang with the guys and gals who print money! They open concepts and they reinvent the landscape every day. They set the new standard. They are the folks who create the concepts that everyone else steals. After working with these guys for so long, I started to take notice of the commonality or formula if you will. I began writing this formula into my consulting projects and the success was instant. I have owned multiple restaurants and I even began applying this secret in my own businesses and wouldn't you know it... that dull whisper was now screaming in my ear. Propelling me forward, making me more successful in all of my businesses and projects alike. Now I am going to share this with you. And I promise if you follow the steps, listen closely and apply the secrets that I am about to show you, the whisper will become an audible scream that both you and your customers will hear.

Quite simply, this book will blow your mind! Why? Because I am going to give you a ton of free and simple marketing ideas and strategies that work. But with that, I will also share the secret sauce, the recipes, and formulas that make it all work. Period!

I have tried, implemented or done a case study on each and every one of these ideas, either in my restaurants or with the hundreds of projects and clients I have worked with. The ideas you are about to discover will change your mindset, your creative process and your bottom line.

My father was a mechanic, an inventor, a philosopher, an entrepreneur and my best friend in the world! He taught me many lessons but the most important thing he taught me was, "If you give a boy a hammer, the world is his nail." Quite simply put, if you give someone a tool, they can or will try to fix everything with it. If the whole world is a nail and you don't teach someone how to effectively use the tool, they are going to smash up a ton of shit!

Before using any tool you have to have the proper mindset. A hammer can be a weapon or it can be a precision instrument to help you build something amazing. It starts with your mind set. I will cover a lot about mindset throughout this book. You have to believe in yourself, your brand, your people, your product and most importantly you have to believe and understand your purpose.

I am also going to teach you how to use the tool. If you are like most restaurant operators, you are looking for a quick fix. You have to be willing to fix your mindset first. Many books have great ideas but if you're like me, you think they are low on content and worse, they give you a hammer and tell you the world is your nail. But they do not show you how to properly use the tool or the reason why the tool was even developed in the first place.

So... where do we start?

The truth is, most books are structured to inspire but they don't give you a process or a path to implement. That ends right now!

Many operators in this business get stuck with marketing. Either you don't know what it really means to market, you don't know what type of marketing you should do for your business, or you don't know the steps to take to get started. Likely, you have some really big ideas. This book will help you understand all of these things. More importantly, I will provide **YOU** the step by step way to roll it out, track it, measure it and recycle the ones that work while tweaking the ones that don't.

You may have little to no budget for marketing or you are spending money with a company and not happy with the return. Hell, if you are spending money with another company and you are happy with your results, you will still benefit from this book. These are all simple, step by step ideas that will literally print money!

I'm guessing if you picked up this book or downloaded it, you are within the vast majority of restaurants that actually have no budget or a minimal budget for marketing. If that is you, don't worry… you are not alone. I work with over 100 clients a year and I see the same thing with successful and unsuccessful concepts alike. They have no budget because they don't see the use. If they just had a solid idea and a grasp on how to make it print (that means make money), then they would spend money. Especially if they could prove their investment had an ROI (Return on Investment). Does this sound like you? You will not have an **excuse** after you read this book. I encourage you to implement as many ideas as you can. When you have a win, send me your success story and I will put your name in lights! I will add your story and print as many successes as I can in the second edition of this book.

Okay, enough of that! Let's light this firecracker!

THE SECRET SAUCE

*Don't only practice your art, but force your way
into its secrets; art deserves that, for it and
knowledge can raise man to the Divine.*
~ Ludwig van Beethoven

There is a secret in business that some of the most successful businesses know. They may not be able to explain it, but they feel it and they allow themselves to be guided by their intuition or their gut. This secret is pervasive and instrumental to their success. This secret is scalable across all business and it applies directly to the marketing, branding, messaging and image of a company. It is one mystery that everyone business seems to be searching for yet it eludes most people. Those that have it can't explain it and those that want it can't seem to find it.

First I must tell you, I am not a writer. I am a restaurant business freak! I am not bound by a writers rules nor do I really care about them. So, true to form let's break from tradition right now.

Instead of stringing you along and doing some impactful, roundabout conclusion in the end of the book the eloquently threads all of the chapters and Ideas together with some life changing conclusion I rather give you all the goods right up front. I think the instant gratification will serve you better and it also enhance the following chapters of this book and help give you a deeper perspective. So here we go...

To begin it is important that I explain the concept of Whisper Marketing. While, sure, this book if full of great, proven, and even measurable marketing ideas, these ideas are only illustrations meant to stimulate and compliment the concept. The real "secret" is in **Whisper Marketing Formula**. The success, effectiveness and sustainability of this formula is much bigger and more important than any single idea in this book.

As the saying goes... *"The whole is indeed greater than the sum of its parts"*.

Whisper Marketing is more than a clever, juxtaposed, title to another marketing book. As the title would intimate, this book is more about this "secret" than it is about the whisper itself. The secret is the real message and the whisper is simply it's vehicle.

I call it Whisper Marketing because that is exactly what it is. Look around at your favorite concept. Whether it is a restaurant, a piece of technology or even a clothing line, regardless of what brand icon you may deem as your favorite... if they are on your radar they are likely a Whisper Marketer.

Whisper Marketing is passive, steady, consistent and woven so deeply into the fabric of a successful brand that they typically do not need to ever sell you a thing. Their marketing seems nonexistent or effortless at best, yet people tend to flock to them and they can't explain why. These "Whisper Marketers" are not overt or aggressively chasing their would be patrons with one dimensional tactics. They don't shout at you. They certainly don't pander! And most importantly, they never, ever apologize. They don't look desperate and they do not sell out.

[The best way I can explain the "sell-out" is this: The apparent desperation oozing out of a confused brand that has decided to become everything to everyone.]

Take a look at brands that you think are less than ideal and see if the "sell-out" definition applies. Take it a step further and ask yourself where your brand falls in this continuum?

So if this has captured your attention then you are ripe to begin learning the dynamic process of what is Whisper Marketing. If your thinking I am going to tell you all of this works by being invested in multiple different investing channels, I'm not. That is not the secret. It may become a practical strategy for some brands but this secret is much deeper and more profound than that.

Over my 25 year career in the hospitality field the past 15 have been intensely spent studying, interviewing, observing and absorbing what the best in the industry do and how they have become so successful.

I knew it in principle for years before I could even explain it. There truly is a secret code to marketing and while it many seem simple in theory, it turns out it is really quite challenging to digest it and then later capture and explain it.

It is important first that I qualify the true genesis of successful concepts. I am not talking about the ones that you see with the private equity behind them with hoards of cash. You know those big national brands with an immeasurable budget and bottomless pockets. The ones that blare through every TV and Radio ad know to man, the ones advertised in all the traditional channels through pure exhaustible saturation marketing. Nor is it the multi-unit concept with annoying pop-up ads all throughout the inter-webs deeply discounting their products.

While these brands do have "effective" marketing relative to saturation and visibility, the strategy if so foreboding and their acquisition cost per customer is so exorbitant that they have dug themselves into an hole so deep that they may never get out. This hole only gets deeper due to the inherent nature of risk aversion that has been created by the expectations they have allowed their customers and their investors alike. I am sure you can think of a few big brands that might fit this description. These brands are the antithesis of the Whisper Marketers and seeing where these big brands have wrong and how to avoid these same pitfalls will make itself very apparent by the end of this chapter.

So, No! These are not the concepts I am talking about at all. At least not in there current state. But believe it or not at the nexus of some these big brand's evolution they could have easily been Whisper Marketers in the beginning but having a lack of awareness of the "Whisper Marketing Concept" allowed them to make, what were otherwise, fatal mistakes without even being conscious of them.

On the other hand, the concepts I am talking about are the

obscure, the out of know where, overnight success concepts that are absolutely just "killing it".

I have had the extreme fortune and pleasure to work with these specific clients for the past 15 years. The guys and gals who are known by name in the inter-circles of the snobbiest of food snobs. The coinsures of creative concepts, the foodies (Here's another secret: The word Foodie is a terrible word that is rejected and considered insulting to anyone that is truly a "Foodie", by the way.)

These concepts are edgy. They push the envelope. They take, what on the outside, looks like such an incredible risk (so much so that when duplicated, these would be copycats fail capture the same result and become quick to dismiss the luck of these disruptive brands as simply fortuitous concepts) … "They were just in the right place at the right time", they will say…

- But "they" are wrong!

A knock off is a knock off and they don't often work because the most critical element of the replication is missing. This element is above and beyond any exterior veneer or a clever menu or even a cool image. For these exceptional breakout concepts it is the understated, unidentifiable core element that is often overlooked or just simply missed during any kind of replication process. This key element is affectionately know as passion or, as I like to call it, "Purpose".

These concepts live their passion on purpose with purpose. Truth be told, it doesn't even have to be a remarkable

14

purpose to anyone else but it is indeed remarkable, necessary and needed by and from its creator.

This can manifest itself in so many ways but genuinely the best of the best do not shout out their purpose. Instead it is simply a static, continuous, unflinching way of life. It is humbling for an artist to brag about their success and even harder much of the time for them to explain ho this process works. But it is also engaging for them to be able to passionately share this purpose with anyone who picks up on the subtle nuance and can ask the right questions.

This concept is hard to grasp, for reasons that will be made clear shortly, but it is not a hard one to execute once it is understood and embraced. While I have been on a quest the better part of my career to capture this concept, I was able to execute against it long before I could explain it beyond just saying "trust me, I know this works". In the case study below, I was forced to get better at explaining it and why the "trust me, I know this works" wouldn't be enough in this case.

CASE STUDY
"DEL ROSSO'S - Organic Italian Kitchen"
Whisper Marketing Concept

I was working with a large, multi unit concept that I will call "Del Rosso's - Organic Italian Kitchen".

Del Rosso's had been in business for 10 years and had up to 5 locations at one point. They had experienced some great initial success in the beginning years of their operation. They had even franchised a few stores. By the time I was brought in to work with the group they had bought back the franchise locations and had to close one. Sales were in a tailspin and the concept was trying everything in their power to get back to their "golden age" of previously realized success.

The big challenge I had was discovering what changed. What was different from the early success to where they were now?

In my research and interviews I had discovered how confused the brand was and how they allowed themselves to get there.

Del Rosso's started in the very early stages of the organic craze circa 2005. Their early success resonated with both them and their clientele. But the brand had no rules (I will explain that in just a moment). The early identification, as realized by the owner, was that people wanted good, clean, healthful alternatives to the less than wholesome food in the marketplace and this buzz was on it's way to becoming and audible cry from their consumer base.

As the concept grew they started to lose favor and sales started to slip. It may have been due to the economy (doubtful) or it may have been due to other competitors catching up (also doubtful). In my research I had noticed something else. I noticed a brand with some early initial success that deviated from the core of the brand and allowed themselves to get off the path that had brought them their earlier success. Don't get me wrong, the concept wasn't failing. It was still good but good but good was a far cry from the initial greatness the brand had experienced early.

When the sales did start to slip "Del Rosso's" had identified that while their initial success started with organic foods the landscape was changing. All of the sudden the focus was less about organic foods in the marketplace and the trend towards gluten free options started gaining steam. Being the early adopters that they were, they jumped all over this concept. They worked tirelessly to enter the market with a great gluten free pizza crust and shortly there after they were the "first to market", serving gourmet gluten free pizza. It had seemed they had captured lightening in a bottle once again and the brand began to surge again. The gluten free crust was really quite good and now people had a more expanded option when it came to eating quality, gourmet, organic, gluten free, Italian food.

Del Rosso's became so popular that this helped them go from 2 stores to 3 and it also helped them sell their first 2 franchises. This success had reaffirmed a good result but unfortunately it was one derived from a bad conclusion. More on that in a minute.

Some time later the sales started slipping again. I am told again that "the competition had caught up", "the customers started focusing on different things" and in order for them to stay on track they would once again needed to chase the "trend du jour" and get in front of it. And once again they did.

This time it was all about the sustainable food. The local, farm to table movement. So, true to form, Del Rosso's did their due diligence. They searched the local market for farm to table product. They worked on new recipes and when they were ready they unveiled their new and improved menu. This time, they even kicked it up a notch. This was the state I found them in and this is what I was greeted with upon my first visit to one of the locations...

The outside sign still said **"DEL ROSSO'S - Organic Italian Kitchen"**. The environment was very cool and trendy on the inside. The interior was artfully done with trendy design elements and thoughtful layout. The first impression was promising. Then I got the menu...

The cover of the menu was watermarked with every buzzword you could possibly imagine. The intentionally faded words fell behind the logo on the front cover of the menu and they flowed in an angled pattern that took up the entire page. The background cover was filled with the following words of different sizes and fonts calling out the brand focus.

"Farm to Table", "Gluten Free", "Organic", Sustainable", "Vegan", "Allergy Friendly", "Gourmet", "Non-GMO", "Local" and likely some others I can't recall.

How does that sound to you? To me, it was confusing as hell! To me, they had committed the "cardinal sin" that no brand should ever commit... they had tried to become everything to everyone. Like most consumers, I couldn't understand how they could do all of this and be good at any of it but I was cautiously optimistic and eager to give it a shot.

Upon my first visit they must have thought me a pig. The staff had no idea I was there on a reconnaissance mission so imagine my servers arched eyebrow when I order 5 different items off of this gigantic menu. It was even more confusing when I my meatball appetizer came topped with sriracha slaw and was accompanied by vegan, organic, gluten free bread.

Huh?

Asian slaw on top of an Italian meatball dish? Vegan bread with a meat dish? What the hell was going on here? And then it hit me. Not only were they trying to be everything to everyone and jumping on the bandwagon of every buzz worthy product and food trend known to man, they had also exceeded their boundaries of Italian and moved into the dreaded "fusion" world.

The brand had lost it's way and that is because the initial outline for the brand was not the brands rules but rather just something cute and current that the brand used as a tag line.

Rules? What rules? If I have lost you, let me back up. The rules of the brand are typically delivered at inception. What you will later learn in this book is the concept of the USP or "Unique Selling Proposition". This is your brand's tag line. The tag line or USP is not just a way to differentiate yourself or describe yourself. It is, in fact, the premise for your brands position and the first elements used to create your brand's rules.

Let me illiterate the example of **Del Rosso's Organic Italian Kitchen**.

The words "Organic", "Italian" and "Kitchen" become the guiderails for the brands rules.

If we break down each word of the brand we can create rules and these rules should require a strong constitution, regardless of what is happening in the environment around you.

Organic: The word organic is a big word to use on a concept. It would intimate that everything on the menu is organic. That is fine if indeed that brand adheres to that rule. Del Rosso's did not. Some of the things were organic but as I was later told, they couldn't source an entire menu that was organic.

"Uhhhh, then don't put that up in lights…maybe?" I thought out loud.

You are not being true to who you say you are and that will, at a minimum, confuse a customer or worse, it will disappoint them.

Italian: Everything then should be Italian, correct? Apparently not. The menu in its current state had evolved to include Asian, American, Italian, Fusion and maybe even some French undertones with a dribble of Spanish influence smattered here and there.

Again I ask, "WHAT?!?!"

And again, it is confusing to the customers.

Kitchen: A worthless word that tells me nothing about the brand other than it is a restaurant. It is redundant and it takes up space. It doesn't add anything to the brand so why is it in the tag line? The customer doesn't need to know that it is a kitchen. The online look up of restaurants in the area and even the patio tables and the umbrellas did a sufficient enough job of giving that part away.

In my initial, objective, observational report back to the leadership team I met with strong resistance. This is predictable and I get it. A concept is very personal and one with a lot of emotional attachment. We put our money, blood, sweat and tears into our concepts. Our brand is often "our baby" and having owned multiple restaurants myself, nobody knows that more than me. But this was not an attack on the baby. I was not slapping the baby but I was certainly slapping the parent.

The concept came to me because they were broken and tanking and they didn't know why. The why became very apparent in short order.

The brand was breaking so many rules. The menu was too big to execute, which required too many different product skews on hand. This stretched their ability to scale and to buy product the right way. This, in turn, led to having too many different ingredients on hand which later gave way to their inability to manage the quality of the product. That manifested itself in the form of waste and having to buy smaller pack sizes which led to higher prices which also led

them to have to price themselves out of the market. All of this combined devolved to a lower quality of food both in the handling of the product and the execution of consistent thoughtful product going out to the guest. Because, after all, how can the best cook in the world manage over 120 different menu items and do any of them well?

With all of that combined Del Rosso's now had an abundance of staff in the kitchen in order to manage this craziness which absolutely killed the labor cost thus forcing the brand to raise the menu price even more which in the end left the brand with a lopsided, confusing, over priced bad value proposition to the guest... and yet they couldn't understand why the sales were slumping and why the profitability was so terrible.
To them their arguments and their logic was sound and likely even proven.

When sales began to drop they had realized early success by jumping on the "food trend du jour" and by adding it to their repertoire, it would enhance the brand and systematically impact their sales in a positive way.

Were they wrong? After all, this had been their vehicle for success.

In order to answer the question I had to hold them accountable to their desired outcome. The outcome they had expressed to me when bringing me on board was one of restoring their profitability and helping them get back on track with a sustainable, scalable brand for continued growth. If that is the desired outcome than it would be easy for me to hold them accountable to the actions needed to create that outcome. If the outcome was different than they would need to explain it to me.

The group agreed, this was indeed their desired outcome.

So we started our first exercise. I asked each member of their executive team (6 in total) to pick three words or phrases to describe their brand.

"These descriptors need to be clear, concise and synonymous with the brand throughout", I instructed.

"They don't have to be current, however. You can describe the brand to me as you think it should be, what it was, what it could be or what it is. It doesn't matter, just so long as you all give me a thoughtful answer."
They were all over the place.

The principal thought the focus should still be all about "Organic Gourmet Italian".

The second in command thought it was "Gluten Free, All Natural, Italian".

The subsequent members of the team all had different answers and about all they could agree on was Italian.

It was unbearable but at least it was a start.

My reframe then was two fold. First it was important to illustrate to the team that not only was the brand confusing

to the guest, but second (it was clear) it was also confusing to their own team. And that led me to help Del Rosso's grasp the secret that is Whisper Marketing.

[In Whisper Marketing there is a nucleus that is paramount

to a brands success and then there are three core tenants that protect and enhance that nucleus. And so I explained...]

In order to be able to Market your brand successfully you need to understand your brand. When you understand your brand and you can successfully explain it, you will be able to ask yourself, "Who will this brand appeal to?"

This will lead you to be able to identify your audience or demographic) so you know where to spend your time, money and efforts.

Understanding your brand is "The Nucleus" and that at its core is the brands Purpose!

Then there are the Core-3 or what I call the 3 C's – Clarity, Continuity and Consistency.

My first question to the group following are little "describe the brand" exercise was about the brands Purpose.

Me: "When you started this company you hit the ground running with amazing fanfare. The concept grew and it was profitable. What was the need that you identified early that caused you to say this was necessary in the market place? What was it that caused you to risk your financial

security due to what you were so sure was missing in your landscape that it seemed like a no brainer? Can you explain that to me?

The Principal: "I was sick of living in a city that didn't have one great Italian Restaurants. As an investor I have traveled all over the world and experienced some of the greatest food. I wanted that for our town. In my travels to Europe, I also noticed the great care they took for food and how healthy the locals looked. The food was unadulterated, clean, simple and well techniqued. So in 2005 I set out on a mission to bring that to my city. It was received well and we took off."

Me: "Wow! I am inspired! I want to eat there." I said. "So what happen to that place?" I asked.

Principal: "This is that place!"

Me: "Is it? Because I don't see that here. I don't even see a trace of that here."

I then explained my earlier diatribe about how out of control that place had gotten, how far removed from the initial purpose it had deviated and what this has all led to. I continued on with my observation of how his travel and experience of good food, while charming, was causing him to deviate even further from his brand when he would come home from abroad and regale his men in the amazing food he had eaten in Japan or Spain and how they needed to add this or that to their menu because it was so amazing.

"That is not how you pick a new item", I told him, "that is

how you pick a new concept".

There is nothing wrong with wanting to duplicate his original purpose and apply the same logic to different regional offerings of food but he would need to do so with a different brand. If it is not Italian than either change the name on the outside of the building or don't add the item.

And this is how we start to identify and use our rules.

The light bulb went off and they started to get it. We had regained an understanding of the nucleus and I think it might have been the first time the people in his organization heard and clearly understood the genesis and purpose of the concept. And it didn't come from me, it came from their leader.

Me: Can we agree that the brand needs to find it's original purpose again?"

The team: "Yes"

Me: "Can we agree that the brand will need to have rules and that those rules will be the rules by which the concept is governed?

The team: "yes!"

Me: "Can we agree that whatever those rules are that you will allow them to hold you accountable to how you manage this brand?"

And the answer was…**"YES!"**

Del Rosso's had just experienced an epiphany and they had just unlocked the mindset needed to recapture their brand and for the first time in years. As it was explained to me by the second in command, they were all on the same page and it felt good!

Del Rosso's was ready to start their path towards success and to learn how to use the Whisper Marketing concept to help them get there.

The first thing we had to do as a group was to re-identify what the brands purpose is?

Is it still the same as it was in the beginning?

Does it need to be modified, changed or stay the same?

Or does the brand need to be completely reimagined?

The group decided that for the most part the original purpose was right. So we worked on an exercise to create a statement that was short and to the point. What is the purpose? (This technique will be revealed in a later chapter when we discuss the concept of the "elevator pitch").

Ultimately, the defined purpose of the brand was this:

"A conscious, community driven brand dedicated to clean, healthy and flavorful Italian cuisine."

This would be the overarching theme of the brand. It didn't need to written on a wall or on a business card. Instead it needed to be embraced, practiced, taught, trained and on display in a way that Del Rosso's would not tell but instead show: their staff, their guests, and their community. This would be their Purpose!

This was above all else their new doctrine. And this doctrine would have to have a story and that story would have to be supported by the reason for its existence.

The next part of the exercise requires context.

Great story! It sounds like fluffy marketing B.S. As a guest or member of the community, or even a member of your staff, why should we care about this? Why do we need this? They would have to explain this and explain this they did…

"It is needed because we live in a world where short cuts are the norm. Where big business set the food edict and profit is king. We allow ourselves and our family's principles to be compromised at the expense of our health and wellness for the sake of convenience and price. In a world where big corporations are quick to fortify our diets with quantity over quality and volume over value. We need someone who will stand up for wholesome food. We need a movement that will fight back against how our recklessness towards the food that is killing us. We need a safe place where communities and their people can trust their food and their food sources so that we can live a better and more healthful life. We need to care for people if we expect people to care. That is why we are needed and that is why we are relevant."

The passion that came form this mission statement made me want to try the food again. I was blown away!

But now that we had this "Mission Statement" how would we let people know? Like any other introduction you will have a short, medium and long explanation about yourself to your audience. Nobody wants the "life story" in the initial introduction. When someone is introduced they are looking for the quick introduction. If they like what they hear they will be inclined to dig a little bit deeper and if they still like what they hear they will want more.

[Consider courting a new customer in the same way your would court someone you want to have a personal relationship with. If the first impression doesn't appeal to them, let them move on. You will have wasted neither too much of your time or theirs. This will give both parties the ability to look for a better match and with more time to do so, both parties will have a higher likelihood of succeeding in reaching the audience they really want.]

THE BREIF INTRODUCTION
Next we had to be able to take all of this language and turn it into our USP (Unique Selling Proposition).

"What are the three words or phrases that will really capture this and put on display so that the world can see?" I asked the group.

The Del Rosso's team and I put our heads together to figure out how or what 3 words or phrases would position our purpose and give some insight to what we are all about and be in direct alignment with the mission statement. And here is what we came up with.

DEL ROSSO'S - Healthy, Modern, Italian.

Now we had something serious to work with.

Healthy: This is a beautiful and slightly ambiguous word this gives us a lot of freedom. The "food focus du jour" would make sense in this context without us having to look so desperate and jump on every bandwagon issue that comes up as the evolution of food and the consumer focus changes. One thing is true, the bigger emphasis behind all of these buzz words floating out there in the ether are largely rooted in health. Nutrition, Non-GMO, Gluten Free, Organic… and the list goes on and on. But we are not pigeonholed to just one word like before with "Organic". As opposed to Organic, where the expectation was that everything would be organic, we now had a little bit more wiggle room. This became one of the first qualifying rules for the food. It would have to be healthy.

Modern: Modern is also one of those ambiguous words that gives the brand some freedom and creative liberty that would be critical. If the opposite of modern is traditional then we were better served using this word because Del Rosso's was anything but traditional. Additionally, Modern and Healthy are complimentary in the juxtaposed assumption or association that goes hand in hand with

"traditional Italian cuisine". Most "traditional Italian food" elicits descriptors like: heavy, rich, pasta, dense, red sauce, filling, etc. So to position the brand as "Healthy, Modern, Italian" we would be sending a message that breaks free from the traditional expectation of the "traditional Italian Restaurant". The word modern would also insulate some of the creative elements of Del Rosso's menu. It would give the culinary team opportunities to be creative and create separation from the other guys. And best of all, the guest shouldn't be surprised because not only does it not say "Traditional Italian" it delivers an expectation to the guest that it will go beyond that with something new and different.

Italian: As a third descriptor we felt that this was better than kitchen because it actually gave a clear and definitive position on the food expectation. I still don't know what the hell the purpose of using the word kitchen was in the former iteration.

We also selected these three words in order of importance. It was clear to me that the brand had more focus on the healthful elements of the concept and "Healthy" would be the lead element of the message over anything else. Next was the "Modern".

We could have put modern in front but it isn't what the brand leads with. The brand was more about the gluten free, organic and natural overtones on the menu than it was about the creativity or newness of its offering.

While the conclusion and description might sound easy, I assure it wasn't. It took quite a bit of time to get everyone on the same page and there was a lot of back and forth but eventually we got there and then that became the infrastructure needed to begin working on the rules. This would prove to be harder still. While the rules themselves were not the hardest thing to create, the adherence and eventual accountability to these rules would be a whole other story.

THE RULES

Like I said, the rules are pretty simple at this point. If we have said all of these things that we are then all we have to do is look at our environment and ask one simple question relative to every element in the business.

Does this enhance or compliment who we say we are or does it have a negative or competing value against who we say we are?

This part of the process can be very emotional. We all have things that we are in love with when it comes to our concept. And unfortunately with the absence of rules we allow our personal brand and preferences (things we like) to infect our private brand (the concept). With great rules and foresight this can be done in harmony and it can work well to compliment a persona and a product seamlessly but when it is unintentional and later has to be called to task it can be very hard to undo.

As an opening exercise I decided not pull any punches. I wanted to attack the most coveted thing in the restaurant right away. And that was the menu. How personal would you be willing to guess that was?

Well, the answer was very, very personal. I was yelling at them and they were yelling at me and before you knew it they were ready to abandon their rules for the sake of an emotional attachment or worse because of fear.

The reason why this exercise created so much fear is because they had data telling them our decisions about cutting menu items was wrong or at a minimum conflicting. The GM of the busiest location had printed a "Product Mix Sales Report" and was using it as a crutch. Every time we would decide to kill an item, he would say, "We can't, it's too popular" or "its one of our best sellers", followed by, "people will revolt!"

- To which I could only say,

"The consequences of your previous actions have zero impact on doing what we need to do to make this brand work. Yes, you will get fall out and that will be the hardest part of this exercise for anyone. Cutting off the foot to save the leg is hard! It is very, very hard. But that doesn't mean it is not necessary."

- Crickets…

I continued, "Trust me, I get it, I really do! I am asking you to take a very large risk. You might think it doesn't effect me because I am not vested in your company. You are right in assuming that is doesn't effect me. But not because it I'm not vested. I am extremely vested, every client I work with will dictate the outcome of my career. If I fail, I have no clients, if I succeed, I have more clients. The harder the job, the better the next job and the inverse is true as well. You see, I am not effected by the fallout of this because I know it is a risk that will pay off. And I know that because I have done it, multiple times. You guys have deviated so far down a road that while it disconnected with a large majority of people, it still has a strong loyalty to others and the position you will have to take in risking pissing off your loyalists is both real but also for the greater good. And I know that is very counter intuitive. But these are your rules. You want the change? You want the "golden age" of this brand restored? I will hold you accountable or I won't be a part of it. You won't be taken seriously as a "Healthy - Modern - Italian" restaurant if you have Asian slaw on your f'ing meatball! You want the cure, you follow the prescription. You don't like the way some of the medicine tastes, that fine! Don't take it but guess what? When your dead I won't be liable for practicing bad medicine. This will be on you for only doing the parts you are comfortable with."

Still crickets...

After about 2 solid minutes of pissed off posturing on both side of the table, not a word spoken, I eventually put my laptop and my notebook back in bag and walked out the door... with my head cocked over my shoulder, I sarcastically wished them good luck.

The next day, I got a phone call from the owner. As cooler heads prevailed we came back to the table.

I opened with accountability. Illustrating that I did not write their "Purpose" or their mission statement nor did I define their USP. I facilitated the conversation because I knew the direction and outcome needed but at the end of the day the conclusion and the content was there own. I asked for assurance and acceptance from the group that this is indeed how it happened and when they all agreed I continued.

"All of this stuff that you said is who you are and who you need to be will become your rules. If you cannot be true to those ideas and accountable to them you are wasting my time and yours. I would recommended you save yourself the time, money and anguish right now and walk away. Go get a job at someone else's restaurant and waste their money. Seriously, sell this business right now while it is still worth something, otherwise you will continue to run it into the ground and that will be the end of that. And I will not have my name associated with something like this. Understood?"

And once again, Jiminy F'ing crickets...

So I continued, "Gentlemen, I need an answer! Are we going to move forward together or go our separate ways?"

The principle nodded his head and it was agreed by everyone that we would move forward. As we got back to the menu we started at the top and moved our way down. It was an absolute butcher job.

Each menu item would go through the same exact firing squad of questions.

"The answer needs to be yes to all three", I would say, before calling out the items name.

"Is it Healthy? Is it Modern? Is it Italian?"

If the answer was, "no" to any of these three elements, we would use what is called a "decision tree".

The follow up to a "no" was simple. Can we make it a "yes"? Meaning could we modify the item to fit our three element "yes rule"? If the answer was still "no", then it was cut.

The menu was over 116 items. By the end of the first part of the exercise we had 72 items left.

That was good but we needed to shoot for 60 items.

[As a rule, the larger the menu the cheaper the price and more expensive the food. This concept is supported by a study titled "Goal Dilution" by Ayelet Fishbach and it the premise for menu size valuation. Basically, the cost of goods go up because you have to buy too many items to support the large menu which in turn minimizes the ability to buy everything in bulk. The price is lower because the consumer's confidence is lost when a menu surpasses 64 items. That is the point at which the menu feels too big and the consumer's value proposition says, "I will expect to pay less if the menu is too large because I don't have faith the food will be "world class" and if it isn't the best it better be the cheapest". For the guest, perception is reality. And if we ever put our guests in a position of questioning us we have already failed them. I will digress but I will also shamelessly plug my book called "On the Menu" which has all the science, value proposition and sociology of the menu with case studies, rules and details about managing, building and engineering a world class menu with maximized profitability.]

After butchering the menu we had to move on the every other aesthetic in the restaurant.
Does the physical menu answer the question. Does it represent "Healthy – Modern – Italian"?

How about the décor? The uniforms? The training? And so on and so forth. Believe it or not, the menu ended up being the hardest part of all the exercises.

Wow! That's a lot to take in right? Probably, but that is not the point. Again, the Whisper Marketing concept is the anthem but we don't have to sing it or shout it on high. Instead we have to live it and it needs to be synonymous through the brand.

The people that need to hear the story are the people that want to hear this story. And believe me, there are people that want to hear this story. No, not everyone has to hear this story and that's okay. Everyone is not your market. But those that care passionately about this message will be your viral audience. Your passionate audience that believes in you and your cause. And these people will become your tipping point or your initial catalyst for your Whisper Marketing movement.

There are also those people who work for the organization, they want to (and need to) hear this. If you think you live in a world where employees and customers are loyal to a company, than you are crazy!

There is nor more loyalty to companies there are only loyalties to causes. If the company is the cause and the cause the company then you have purpose. And if you live it, eat it, breath it and believe in it, with blind and unrelenting devotion… then you reap the rewards from it.

If, on the other hand, your company has a week constitution or an unclear or undefined cause, or worse, one that is nothing more than a thinly veiled attempt at placating an audience with a fluffy marketing agenda.. you might come out of the blocks strong but you will eventually be exposed. And that will begin your companies cycle of stasis which will eventually lead to its death.

And lastly, if this great cause should ever be abandoned, changed or if it should waiver over the course of the companies growth and evolution than you should expect that eventually so to will its audience.

Consider all of that and now reflect back on our earlier conversation about those big "soulless" brands that fail to resonate with anybody because they are trying so hard to resonate with everybody.

This is the secret. Everything else is structure, rules, ideas and implementation.

Achieving this outcome is not easy and like any secret when you are given the code or the blueprint, the instruction manual or the process it may make you smarter but it is worthless if:

- **You can't grasp and trust the concept**
- **You don't follow it exactly as a formula**

My team and I have one of the most impressive resumes in the industry when it comes to turning brands around and helping them achieve massive growth. When it comes to building and developing sales and marketing strategies we change the overall outcome of good businesses and make them great.

As a consultant, I guarantee my work, outcomes and plans 100%. And guess what happens when my programs don't work? The outcome simply boils down to our clients not being able to break from their risk aversion tactics enough to implement the entire plan. When people ask for a remedy and only take the portions that they are comfortable with and the program fails, it becomes a self-affirming, self-fulfilling prophecy if the clients don't believe in the process. The truth is you can be right or wrong about anything you want to be right or wrong about. Henry Ford had a great quote where he said "Whether you think you can or you think you can't, you are probably right."

The knowledge might be helpful but the reality is all of the secret codes, systems, formulas and processes alike will not get you from here to there. While this marketing secret is indeed a secret, it is not coveted. It is not a closed system of knowledge by nature (or least not close intentionally) but like most things, those that have discovered how to do it are a little more artistic by nature and are too busy enjoying their own success to take a moment out to try and capture and explain their system.

The approach to this book and the education that you will be able to extract from it is layout out in a matter that I think will make the most sense relative to educating you as well as defining and describing the steps to go from understanding to implementation and then to execution and replication. Along the way we will also compliment this art with the appropriate blend of science. Marketing is historically a hard thing to measure and none of these teachings will pass muster unless I can prove them out. And so, beyond the ideas and the how to, the execution will also require a measurability in order to protect our interests mutually. I want this to work for you as much as it has worked for me and others.

Now that we have the hard part out of the way we have to move into the practical application of the Whisper Marketing Concept.

A QUICK NOTE:

*I am very passionate about this business and very competitive when it comes to winning. When I don't win I get upset. I obsess about losses and failure. But I also get introspective. I look at what **I DID** first to see what I could have done better. I look to analyze how I failed my client. I accept my failures and I speak to my constituency of trusted advisors and mentors and I unashamedly tell them the whole story, never to spare my own ego. I know if I can't get better then I will stagnate. It is easy to blame the environment, the customer, the timing etc. And trust me, as long as I have been doing this I have heard more excuses than you could imagine. We failed because of our competition. We failed because of the economy. We failed because of a bad review… and the list goes on and on. But it is all bullshit! We fail because we are not accountable to ourselves. We fail because we give up. If you never quit you never fail.*

So at the end of the day when I am accountable to myself I get better and the people around me get better. And there are only three cycles in life. Growth – Stasis – Death. To me there is only one of those that is desirable. I do not want to die or stagnate so I guess for me, growth is the only option. I am abrasive because I have noticed that when I don't speak up when I identify a problem I allow that problem a vehicle for growth. There is only one acceptable cycle for problems to exist in and it is not growth or stasis.

I understand my tone may have come through as harsh and many of you reading may not like my delivery and that is okay. The first rule as a consultant is that of truth. If you are familiar with the famous screaming Chef or Bar Rescuer, you might think these guys yell and scream for ratings. You might think them assholes with huge egos that get off on being rude and belittling people. I may agreed with you when I first started consulting. I was sure you could attract more flies with honey and that all of this yelling was Hollywood hype but I am here to tell you, it is not. The first position in helping anyone is in helping them break free from their shackled mind set. We scream and insult and yell and berate people because the message is not getting through. If you give me lip service and just agree with me to get me off your back then I have failed. In my early career I was soft and

submissive and that would lead to people telling me that they understood but they did not demonstrate to me that they understood. That would later lead to me giving a team a great plan complete with the steps and logic but because the team didn't understand, embrace, or agree with the logic, they would fall back into their old pattern and only implement bits and pieces of the plan. This would later lead them to tell me that the plan had failed and they have gone back to doing things how they use to do them. And without fail, in short order, the business would fail.

I tell the story of "Del Rosso's - Organic Italian Kitchen" not to pick on them (not their real name by the way) but because they are such a perfect illustration of so much of what not do and because of that they likely represent one or more challenges and failures that so many brands go through. In fact they might be the one client that did so much wrong collectively and some how stayed alive long enough, that in spite of themselves, to be bale to finally give in a be open makes them a perfect illustration for this introduction. They risked a lot and had to be vulnerable and open in order to keep their dream and business alive. Not just alive (that is stasis, the step before death) but thriving and growing.

YOU WILL FAIL...

"Whether you think you can or you think you can't, you're probably right!"
~ Henry Ford

How's that for a chapter title? Funny, but the truth is... you will fail, if you do nothing. The number one reason people fail is because they do not take action! I will not even take on a client if they cannot prove to me in the first day that they have a track record of implementation and that they are willing to take action. You have to be willing to fail. Failure does not describe a person, it describes an event. You are not a failure if you do; you are only that much closer to figuring out how to win by figuring out what not to do. You can even shorten the learning the curve by doing exactly what you are doing right now. By trying to gain insight and understanding in other's learnings and lessons.

The truth about marketing is... "You will fail". The failures are not big and some times they are not even about failing but about how much better the outcome or result could have been if you did it differently. That insight only comes from doing it.

I have had so many failing ideas in business, events, concepts, relationships, and the list goes on and on. However, I am terribly successful and sought out by the masses because of my success. I advertise my successes and I learn from my failures. One of the best things I was ever taught was this…

"FAIL FORWARD FAST!"

Here's what that means, take action on an idea quickly, fail and learn from it. Then improve upon it and do it again as soon as you can. Of course you don't do it the same exact way. Figure out where it failed or where you think it failed and try, try again.

In marketing the principle of failure is one of the biggest money making strategies the world has ever known. It isn't called failing, it is called split testing. Whereby you try an idea multiple different way to see which ones wins out the best. I am not going to dive in to that level of marketing here and now, but I will leave you with the simple premise. You have an idea, then you try it multiple ways to see which way was the most effective. When you find that best way, it becomes the rule for the next method you try. Google "split testing" if you want more ideas.

If you are starting to get a theme or picture that this chapter is about mindset, you are right! If you didn't notice, don't worry, you'll catch up. There are countless stories of failures in business. As a society, we seem to ignore the failure and celebrate only the success. That is how unimportant failure is. But we must always be intent on learning the lesson of that which failed. Here are failures and success that illustrate this point.

Charles Schultz of Starbucks was rejected over 100 times before he received the financing to build his Starbucks empire.

Steve Jobs was fired from Apple before retaking it and making it the brand that now lives in 1 of 2 households in the US.

Thomas Edison failed hundreds of times before coming up with a working light bulb.

The Post-It-Note was born from a failure, while trying to come up with successful glue that would be stronger than anything on the market. That failed and instead they only came up with a glue that wouldn't cure. Instead of abandoning the glue, they found a way to use a glue that wouldn't cure and use it to their advantage. Not curing meant it wouldn't take the paint off of a wall. So they decided to apply the adhesive to paper that you could post a note on and stick and re-stick anywhere you like.

Henry Ford presented, started and funded his company 3 times and failed before finally coming up with the idea of the automotive assembly line and thus the Ford Motor Company was born.

Walt Disney was fired from a newspaper for having no creativity.

- And of course…

Michael Jordan was cut from his high school basketball team before he finally became the "Jump Man".

What all of these people and products have in common, other than being in the minority, is that they didn't give up. They knew that they would change the world.

Steve Job's paraphrased it best from an excerpt in an apple computer ad by saying, ***"Those that are crazy enough to think they can change the world, are the ones who do."***

Now, we may not be talking about changing **the world** but we are talking about changing **your world**? That seems like a small enough goal to accomplish, yeah?

Here's the deal, I am going to change the world according to the restaurant business. I will make operators more successful; I will put them in the chair on the beach drinking their cocktail of choice. I will make them realize their dreams of owning multiple units. I will make them more profitable. I will give them more time to spend with their families, traveling, developing their passions, etc. because I am crazy enough to believe I CAN! To take from my favorite movie "The Matrix",

Trinity: *"Neo... nobody has ever done this before."*

Neo: *"I know. That's why it's going to work."*

Fix your mindset first. Be motivated to know **YOU CAN!** Remember, there is no "TRY", there is only do or don't

46

do. Take action and implement! To quote the Matrix one last time (I swear).

IN CONTEXT:
While watching one of the child prodigies, Neo sees him focusing his gaze on a spoon he is holding in his hand. The spoon folds over like it were rubber. Neo picks up the spoon and tries to do the same. It doesn't work. Another child gives him this advise.

"Do not try and bend the spoon (with your mind). That's impossible! Instead... only try to realize the truth... There is no spoon... Then you'll see that it is not the spoon that bends, it is only yourself."

AUTHENTICITY

"Bring the best of your authentic self to every opportunity."
~ John Jantsch

Alright look! The root word of marketing is market. You have to know your market. The only thing more important than knowing your market is knowing yourself. You are your brand and your brand is you. I don't mess around trying to be someone I am not. I have been a pain in the ass for most of the people I have ever worked for. I challenge everything I don't agree with. I question everything I don't understand, I have no filter when it comes to things I don't agree with. I have a voice that needs to be heard and ideas that need to be tested and implemented. I challenge conformity. I challenge rules! In a rapidly evolving society, one that is upgraded by some form of technology or innovation every day, I often wonder why we are playing by the rules written years ago. My father's rules may have applied to business in his generation (maybe) but if they have not been updated or even questioned, how do I know they apply in mine?

I don't give a shit if I appeal to the masses. I am certainly not trying to appeal to my father's generation if they are stuck in the hard and fast rules of yesteryear. I am intentionally unconventional. This is my authenticity. It may not appeal to you. I do not apologize for who I am and how I think. There are over 7 billion people on the planet and some of them are just like me. Not all of them are however, and I don't care about the ones who are not like me or that can't or won't be open to a different perspective. I care about the ones who are exactly like me! The ones who believe, act, question and think like me. The ones who take action and implement. If this chapter and my language, or this book in general offends you, send me an email and I'll give you your money back. No questions asked. I am happy to give you every dollar you spent because if you are not like me, if you can't think and see things a little differently, this book won't resonate with you and thus I will fail you. I don't need 7+ billion people to buy this book. I need less than one, one thousandth of 1% to buy this book and I can continue on happy and fully financed to achieve my life's purpose. Do you see where I am going with this?

It doesn't really matter what business you are in. The **#1 lesson** for any concepts purpose and one that leads to any good marketing strategy is quite simple…

YOU CAN'T BE EVERYTHING TO EVERYONE!

I opened this book with a few real life marketing examples.

1.) **I wrote an opening chapter different than one you have ever read before. I did something different and it is something I believe in.**

2.) **I offered a money back guarantee. Purchasing without risk is one of the best marketing lessons I have ever learned and one I apply in all of my businesses.**

Likely, if you are still reading this book it is because I have said something that connects with you. If I connect with you, it is because you know that I know YOU and more importantly you know I will not pander to you because I know myself! I have likely been where you are. I have succeeded where you are failing and you trust I will help you based on what I have promised and written so far. If you are still reading, I have accomplished my goal of knowing myself and knowing my audience.

YOU ARE YOUR BRAND

And your brand is you! Branding is a whole other book but I will give this basic premise. Be genuine to yourself. If your brand is not a reflection of you, you will struggle harder to succeed. If you are not passionate about you and your brand, success is also much harder to achieve.

People can sniff through bullshit from "Jump Street". If you are a hillbilly running a fine dining concept, you will fail, not because you are a hillbilly but because you are not being genuine to yourself. Now, I know what you're thinking, "I am genuine to myself." I hope so. Let me put this in to perspective. The number one mistake I see most failing restaurants commit is they are trying to be everything to everyone. Just like the example in chapter one. They started with a simple enough concept and they didn't get what they wanted or they had a customer tell them, you need to have this or that on the menu.

If you have ever let a customer tell you that you need to do this or that to your menu or your concept and you didn't bother to ask them what made them the authority on this, or even worse, you took their advice without question… you are crazy!

Here is a little word on advice, only take advice from people who's outcome or situation you want to emulate. If a successful restaurateur came in and said, you should have this on your menu, or if I came in and said you should have this on your menu… put it on your menu. If the lady at table 4 told you to put a chicken sandwich on your menu because it will attract more people and you did, you are insane.

It all starts with the metaphorical "chicken sandwich"! This is a real to life example as well as a metaphor. I use the chicken sandwich story all the time. It goes something like this…

We got our menu done and it looks pretty good. We have tested everything on the menu and we love it. Let's show it to some people now… And the people say, "Hey there isn't anything light and healthy on your menu, what about the women, women won't come to your restaurant if you don't have a chicken sandwich." You will get all of this logical feedback and so what do you do? You put a chicken sandwich on the menu. But because you were already positioned to roll out the menu and get started you give lip service to the "chicken sandwich" because you didn't have the time, belief or passion for it. And now you have a plain ass, boring chicken sandwich like every other restaurant on the planet. When people come in to your restaurant and see your plain ass chicken sandwich on the menu, they think to themselves…

"Huh?, This is just like every other plain ass boring

restaurant we go to. Let's find another restaurant that isn't plain ass and boring."

Oh wait, it gets better. The cycle continues like this... Your regular customer who loves your plain ass boring restaurant hears you and your partner talking about why business is slow and why sales are off since you opened, and he interjects... "You know what you are missing?", "Mexican food." Everyone loves Mexican food! It's easy to do, it makes sense and it creates a larger offering. Plus, the food cost is cheap! It's all the same shit rolled up a different way and covered in melted cheese. It'll be great!"

And before you know it... you the metaphorical "Greek Restaurant"! You now have a 20 page menu and you are everything to everyone. Congratulations! Now you are sure to get 7.13 billion people to come to your restaurant. Just open the doors and let them flood in.

- But they don't.

- Why?

I think you got it figured out. I hope that my sarcasm was dripping through in that last paragraph. I know I sound harsh and cynical but I am slapping you upside the head now because if you have employed this logic, you are likely wrong. The "be everything to everyone" logic puts you in the worst branding position in the world. When you try to do everything, people know it isn't possible to be everything and your effort will be stigmatized by the consumer public. They know you can't do it all and do it right. They'll be willing to settle for half ass but they will expect you to be the cheapest in the market. You are now in the "low cost" leader category of the market. So guess what happens if you are not the cheapest guy on the street when you employ this strategy? Yup! You have no customers and you are on your way to running this once great idea right into the ground. If this is you, I am sorry! It is not too late to rebrand but that is another book. If this isn't you, worry not my friend; let it be lesson on what not to do.

I am spending so much time talking about these failures to illustrate what I see every day and if I can get in front of someone making a bad decision, we are both better off.

- Our industry is better off.

- Our customers are better off!

So, let's focus on what all of this means. If you are working in your restaurant, you undoubtedly know your customers pretty well. I want you to participate in this 3 part exercise and gain the clarity of a "GURU". Assuming you have a clear purpose like that of "Del Rosso's", you are now ready to move on to the next exercise.

EXERCISE 1.

Answer these questions in the exercise below.

(Ask your employees, they will know the answers.)

1. Who is my current Customer?

What do they like?
What do they hate?
What is their favorite item on my menu?
What do they love about my concept?
How old are they on average?
Are they mostly men or women, or evenly mixed?
What kind of work do they do for a living?
What do they do for fun?
What kind of music do they like?

2. Who is my ideal customer?

What do they like?
What do they hate?
What is their favorite item on any menu?
What do they love about any concept?
How old are they on average?
Are they mostly men or women, or evenly mixed?
What kind of work do they do for a living?
What do they do for fun?
What kind of music do they like?
What do they watch on TV?

3. Who are we?

What do we like?
What do we hate?

What is our favorite item on our menu?
What do we love about our concept?
How old are we?
Are we mostly men or women or evenly mixed?
What do we do for fun?
What kind of music do we like?
What do we watch on TV?

If number one and number 3 match up, you are genuine to yourself and your brand and your customers get it. If they don't match, focus on #3 and you will find #2. I will show you how to market to #2.

Often times, when I work with failing concepts or concepts that are just aren't doing achieving the goals they had forecasted, this is one of the first places we focus. I give them a this simple exercise.

EXERCISE 2.

Imagine who you think is the most amazing person in the world. Someone you have never met but would die for the opportunity to meet. Now let's say you get that chance. You are at an industry event and your "idol" is there. What's better, you have a chance to meet them. They approach you and say "Hi, I'm so and so! What do you do?" And you say, "I own a great restaurant in, whatever area you are located in."

And your idol says… "Wow, that's awesome!" "We love

to eat out, what kind of restaurant is it?"

Right now, you might be imagining this idol of yours actually coming in to your restaurant. You can put there signed picture on the wall that says, "Hey Buddy, loved the food and the staff!" "Keep up the great work!" "Let's get together again soon".
If that is the reaction you were hoping for, you got a little carried away in this dream scenario.

What would you have said? How would you have answered that question?

From your Idol: "What kind of restaurant is it?"

Let me help you with this part a little bit. Your idol likely won't be interested in your business if you can't grab their attention in one or two sentences. Practice this right now and see if you can.

Were you able to describe your restaurant in one impactful sentence? Now ask yourself, did you describe it in a way that made it sound different, better or unique in comparison to any other restaurant out there?

If you are like most people, you probably didn't.

Did you say something like this?

We are a tavern with great food and a fun atmosphere?

- or

We are steakhouse with awesome steaks and strong cocktails.

or

We are a gourmet burger concept with a little something for everyone.

or

We are a Mexican concept with amazing burritos!

If so, do you think that will make your idol say, "WOW! That is awesome. We have been looking for a place like that. I have never heard of a concept like that."

If you answered anything like most people do, than your "idol" will likely smile at you, wish you luck and move on. Never to visit your restaurant, sign a picture and go with you on your next family vacation.

However, I assume the previous response is the type of response you would like. So here is how you make that happen (I can't guarantee the vacation part). By the way, if you haven't realized how your "idol" can be replaced by "your customer" in each of these scenarios, let me point that out right now.

I am going to list the vanilla examples again but this time I am going to put my spin on it.

BAD: We are a tavern with great food and a fun atmosphere?

GOOD: We run a little tavern with 50 rotating local craft beers on tap and food so good it will make you slap your mama!

BAD: We are a steakhouse with awesome steaks and strong cocktails.

GOOD: We are the ONLY Prime Steakhouse in town that serves natural local beef and we are known for our James Bond Martini's. The most impactful place for business, dates and drinks!

BAD: We are a burger concept with a little something for everyone.

GOOD: We do gourmet burgers with a custom blend of brisket, chuck and sirloin and we have adult milkshakes and the most eclectic selection of local craft beers.

And finally,

BAD: We are a Mexican concept with amazing burritos!

GOOD: We do a modern edgy street taco concept that has the best Tacos, Tunes and Tequila in the city!

See any difference? These are all exact before and after I have done with my clients.

THIS IS YOUR "ELEVATOR PTCH" that I eluded to in chapter one. **This is your differentiation strategy. You have to have this!**

When you do, you will be able to describe your concept in a way that makes people curious. If they are not curious, then they are not part of the 7+ billion people in this world that you care about. This will also help you focus on your core marketing and your mindset. With this kind of a description, you will know who your audience is and who your audience is not. It will also help you when it comes time to decide on what you need to focus on. Sure you can do more things than what you talk about but those are not your prime areas of focus. Anyone can focus on three things. What three things make you better, different and more special than anyone else in your direct market? Find those things and build a one to two sentence speech around them. Then you will be able to market around those things and do it better than anyone else.

Here is another exercise I like to do with my clients to convey a point.

EXERCISES 3.

What is your favorite restaurant?

If you had to choose a place, other than yours, to take someone important for either a meeting, a date, an introduction, etc.

- What would you pick?

- "The Cheesecake factory!"…said no one, ever!

If you are like most people, you named a place that is very niche. You could describe them in two sentences, yeah? And that is your favorite, right? Exactly! Now look at your concept and figure out how to make people do that about you.

One of my favorite (better known) concepts is the Hillstone Restaurant Group. I have worked with this concept in the past and I am a believer. There is no other brand that I am aware of that that does "**IT**" better than them. They have concepts like Houston's, Bandera and Gulfstream just to name a few.

They brand themselves as "upscale/casual dining." Kind of played down but here is what they do awesome. They have a small menu (the same for lunch as it is for dinner) in most cases. They do every single thing on their simple little menu more creatively and better than anyone else in their market niche. Not one or two items, every – single - item! I am not a paid spokesperson nor do I have any vested interest in this concept. I am a fan as a consumer. They are usually priced higher than anyone in the market place in their category yet just about every location has a line out the door, every day. They do next to no marketing externally. They are pretty much a word of mouth concept.

How does one of the most expensive concepts in their category have a line out the door every day and sell similar product for more than anyone else?

Because they do it better than anyone else, period! They have no competition.

Do you know who the best people to attack in a business segment are? The people who have no competition.

And while this is the best kind of competitor to attack, it is far from the easiest competitor to attack.

I am not suggesting you change your concept to be exactly like theirs. That will likely result in you failing because chances are, you will not be able to do what they do better than they do it. Chance are you will not be able to capture their purpose as well as they have captured and practiced it for many years. They have been at it longer and have more experience then you do. However, you can model your concept after them in principle and in purpose. Remember don't take advise from people or concepts that you don't envy. Find your inspiration from those that you do.

MARKETING IS EVERYTHING

"… and everything is marketing"
~ Regis McKenna

Seth Godin is an author and a badass, disruptive, marketing machine! If you are not familiar with his work, check it out. He is the author of several books. One of my favorite lines from his writings is a phrase called "Remarkable Marketing". That is to say, anything worth remarking about is remarkable and that is the most effective form of marketing. It is with that in mind that some of my best marketing ideas were born. Throughout this book, I will give you tons of marketing ideas and strategies that embody this very wisdom.

If marketing is everything and everything is marketing, you need to always strive for the remarkable! Make people talk! Blow them away! Deliver the unexpected!

We are just about there. I know you are probably saying, "Where are the ideas?" They are coming but first you need to get "Market Ready".

GETTING MARKET READY

Let me ask you a question? What would be the best possible scenario of a successful marketing campaign? What would that look like to you?

Got your answer?

Great! So here is the $64,000 question. Will you be ready? If you have made it this far, I have no doubt that **YOU ARE AN ACTION DRIVEN PERSON!** You will implement the ideas from this book and when you do, get ready!

You have to be ready for the business because you will only get one chance. Sure good marketing will get them in the door but successful marketing and planning will ensure you keep them coming back for more. Will you have enough people, product, perseverance to get through it? Of course you will!

- What impression will you make on the guest?
- Are they going to get amazing service?
- Is your restaurant clean?
- Are your bathrooms immaculate?
- Is your staff dressed perfectly to reflect your authenticity? Is everyone on the same page?
- Do you have a plan of how you are going to visit and thank all of these guests for giving you a shot?
- Do you have a way to measure the result of your plan so that you can tweak it and/or re-use it later on down the road?

- Are you going to have a meeting every night after the launch of a rollout so that you can go over the wins and losses with your team?

When you do, are you going to figure out how to repeat the wins and fix the losses?

Have you thought to yourself yet... "Oh shit? I wasn't thinking of all that?"

- If so... good!

These are just a few of the things you will need to be prepared for.

If you have ever used a program like Groupon, you might know what to expect when I talk about getting "Market Ready". Did you learn from that experience? Did you learn something other than not wanting to repeat that experience ever again? If not, think back and ask yourself what went wrong and how it could be improved upon.

Groupon and the countless number of knockoff concepts like them have gotten a lot of negative press from friends and fellow restaurateurs alike. Just about everyone I know says the same thing.

"Awe, that sucked! We got our asses kicked at a discount and those people will never returned. What a waste!"

I too have used the Groupon... with tremendous success I

might add. Do you know why I don't think it sucked? Because I was "Market Ready". I knew it was going to kick my ass at a discount and I didn't care because I knew I would capture new customers for life and give a hook-up to my existing customers.

The cynic says, *"Those people suck, coupon shoppers, ya know! They only chase the coupon and they only come when you have one."*

That might be true but is there any accountability on the side of the person who approved this marketing strategy?

- Usually not.

Most people who coupon or Groupon do so out of desperation. Because they do not have the business they want. The customer only comes to them with a coupon or Groupon because that is what they value their experience at. Those customers are basically telling the owner(s) of that concept; the experience is not worth full price. Maybe the staff sucked. Maybe the restaurant has no identity (purpose) and it confused people. Maybe it's filthy and the restaurant turned them off. Maybe the menu was too big or the food wasn't good. It may have been one, none or many of these things but understand this… **THERE IS NO SILVER BULLET!** Better yet, there is no free lunch. You get what you put in to anything, nothing more and nothing less.

RECOMMENDATION

A quick recommendation on when to use Groupon or services like that.

1.) Regardless of what they might tell you, the rules are flexible. The company soliciting you will tell you they have strict rules but they are in sales and the first price is never the real price. If they are motived to sell, they will adjust their rules. When I last did Groupon, they charged 50% of the sale. I got if for 20%.

2.) Use a product like this as an anchor to something else. If you just use it for no reason, people will interpret your weakness. They will think you are overpriced or desperate or possibly even failing. You don't have to have a real reason but you need to have a "because statement". When people see a discount for no good reason, they assume the worst. Give them something so they don't try to think on their own. Make sure your message matches your purpose. Here are a few examples.

   a. "Have we told you lately how much we love you, let us show you". Check out our Groupon offer running on June 8th!

   b. "In honor of our 3 year anniversary we want to give **YOU** a gift". Check out our awesome gift to you running on June 8th!"

   c. "We are so sure you are going to love our new menu; we are putting our money where our mouth is. On Monday June 8th, check out our ad on Groupon!"

These types of concepts will be around for a while so make sure if you use them, you are creating an anchor reason, you negotiate the best deal, and you set parameters you can live with. If you are busy on Fridays and Saturdays, limit the offer to Sunday – Thursday. If you are busy for lunch but not for dinner, make it available for dinner only. You catching my drift? Think it out!

A RANDOM RANT

Before I go into my next diatribe, let me say this about couponing! I believe that discounting your product in traditional mindless ways is one of the worst things you can do. There are some exceptions but there are very few. For example, I wouldn't discount my regular menu items for Happy Hour (Or as I like to market it "Social Hour"). I would have "Social Hour" prices and "Social Hour" portions. They would be different than that on my regular menu. It would be the same variation of the regular menu but not the exact same amount, presentation or price. I would also never give a "BOGO" (Buy one, get one) and I would never give a coupon that says $XX.XX dollars off. I also very rarely use exclusions like $10 off with the purchase of $30. That is cheap and I will show you more effective ways to make your money work for you.

Remember, *"To a boy with a hammer, the world is a nail"*.

Everyone with a hammer has the responsibility of understanding how to use it. If you did make any of these mistakes, take a little time out right now and go back and dissect what went wrong and think about how you could have made it better!

- **Plan your work and work your plan.**
- **Take action!**
- **Get "Market Ready"**

...and believe me, **it will print!**

NOTE: *In the past few years, there have been tons of Groupon-"esque" concepts pop up. They did a good job marketing their brand because I use them by name in this example. It's good to become synonymous with a concept idea. Like Kleenex! Branding can be a very powerful tool when used properly.*

KNOW IT! or NO, IT.

"The true sign of intelligence is not knowledge but imagination."
~ Albert Einstein

You have heard of the "it" factor your whole life. We have even covered "it". "It" is what makes you different, what makes you stand out, what makes you marketable. If you don't have your "it" then you are doing it wrong! Find your "it" and then embellish it.

"IT" is almost always manifested through passion and purpose. Those who have "it" make it seem so simple. Because it is a part of them. It is synonymous with their brand, themselves and who and what they are. If you only have that one thing, being able to fully embrace who and what you are and you will have your "it".

I am going to do something I almost never do. I am going to give you one of my brands. A brand that I still own and trademark but one that is not in operation right now. I will open this brand again soon and when I do, you can come experience my "IT".

EXAMPLE 1. - "IT"
My Restaurant
Hella Burger

I created a concept a few years back called Hella Burger. It was a pretty funny name but it was tied to a culture and it had a purpose. I knew my audience, I knew what my brand was going to be and I knew what I was going to create.

We took up residence in a converted 27' airstream trailer. This was just about the time the Food Truck craze was hitting the west coast.

The airstream was beautiful and shiny and it had a $100k remodel done to turn it into a state of the art kitchen. Best of all, I inherited it from the previous tenant who used it as a snack shack during the construction build out of a very high end residential business park. The snack shack was established by the real estate developer and owner of the development project. The gentleman's name is Peter. Peter is a very eclectic dude. He wanted to make sure that the construction crew and the new tenants had a trendy little place to eat while construction and leasing was finishing up. Peter also owned many restaurants of which I consulted for. He is a very trendy, flashy and purposefully strange guy (hence a $100k build out on a $25k Airstream). This guy doesn't phone in anything or give lip service to any idea, ever! Image and vision to him is a part of his world, the wilder the better… this was a part of his purpose and is my kind of people.

But before I dive into my story, I need to frame the story of Peter. You need to understand Peter and when I am finished with both of these stories; you will understand what I mean by authenticity.

Another consulting client and amazing friend of mine became great friends with Peter and he introduced us. I was already aware of Peter because of what he was doing to build his restaurants. My buddy Mark (the guy who introduced Peter and me) had begun asking me a few months earlier who I thought were the best chefs in town and if I would introduce him. Of course I first asked why and what he told me blew my mind.

Mark explained that he was working with this guy Peter and Peter was going to open 4 new restaurants in a new modern living retail business area. A space with shops, restaurants and businesses that catered to the residential lofts. Peter promised his tenants this vision of awesome shopping, culture and dining with access to a new light-rail transit system that would take the residence anywhere around the city.

Peter was looking for amazing chefs in the market to offer them a deal they couldn't refuse. He would become partners with these chefs. He would let them create their own concept from soup to nuts, design to menu. And these chefs would own a significant portion of the business with no money out of pocket at all. He was basically an angel investor with a big vision looking for amazing people to help him and them realize some amazing goals together. He had a purpose!

Peter loves food. Big. Amazing. Food! Peter also loves passionate people. He has an ability to make them better. He has money, resources, and vision along with a unique and over the top marketing approach to business. To most of us, this would be a dream come true. However, trying to attract these people was a lot harder than one would think.

Mark and I had talked to a number of chefs and unbelievably, people would say no. "NO? Are you kidding me?" Mark and I couldn't believe people were turning this down. We later understood why. First, most people are accustomed to the old rule, "If something sounds too good to be true, it probably is". The second issue is just a predictable value of human nature. We are more motivated by failure than we are by success. We tend to do whatever it takes to not fail vs. doing whatever it takes to succeed. The human brain is wired to "not lose" vs. "to win". It may seem like nuance but there is a big difference. And thus, people turned down this once in a life time opportunity. They would rather have a meager sense of security than an audacious vision for success that had any risk attached.

When people see something that seems too good to be true and they don't understand the motivation behind it, they will generally walk away from the opportunity. You see, the reason Peter was willing to build a custom restaurant for these people with all the costs coming from his pocket while giving the chef's creative freedom and ownership, wasn't because he was crazy or trying to scam them. He quite simply had a vision. He was so married to his vision that he was willing to take big risks because of his desire to win!

Peter saw a hip, trendy residential living atmosphere that would appeal to the DINK's (Duel Income, No Kids). The people with disposable income who wanted nightlife with art, culture, amazing food and great access to the city without being smack dab in the middle of the city. He was willing to go to great lengths to attract these people. In order to attract these people, he had to attract people like them. The bigger the better! People who could start the trend by opening and running the businesses and restaurants in this space. Those people also happen to be local celebrity chefs.

Peter knew if he could bring these big name chefs and trendy spots to life in this living environment, it would have a huge impact on both the price of his residential lofts and occupancy of the residential towers in the space. He also knew if he partnered with these established, big name chefs, his investment would come back around too.

For our first meeting, to begin our consulting discussions, Peter thought we should get to know each other personally first. He invited me to have a cigar and a big steak dinner.

He picked me up in a completely redone, yellow, 1957 Chevy - New York Taxi Cab. Peter is a round nosed, squatty fellow with a round face and a million dollar smile. Instead of hiring a driver, he dressed the part in his brightest inspired, most colorful sweater, diamond crusted Presidential series Rolex and a news boy cap. When he pulled up he shouted from the open window of the drivers seat, "Hey Ronny, get in… the meters runnin"!

That's Peter! Shortly afterwards, we began working on three of his concepts together. At this point he had attracted 3 amazing chefs but he needed some operational and systems help to get these new concepts off the ground.

Peter and I thought much alike but we couldn't be two different people. We were both masters of our craft, a little strange and passionate about our respective visions. And for both of us, those visions had no ceiling.

As time passed and our project was about to reach its successful conclusion, he asked me if I had any thoughts about what to do with the now empty airstream trailer. He had told me that he had promised the now finished retail park business owners and loft residents, four restaurants. He had only delivered three and the fourth was going to take a while due to some engineering challenges within the space. He wanted someone with a great vision, who would want to take over the space and do something unique. He would give them a screaming deal so he could fulfill his promise to his tenants. I knew from past experience and implementation, he really would give someone a screaming deal. And this deal was right up my alley. It was a "remarkable" space. Of course, I would have never spent the money to redo this trailer out of the sheer principle of diminishing returns.

Anyway, I told him I would take it. I presented my business plan (because I always have a handful of business plans that I keep for this kind of occasion). And, as it turned out, I was fresh off of selling a burger concept with my partner in Costa Rica that did very well. A gourmet burger concept was just what our market intelligence told us was needed and it was the gap this retail business space needed as well. We got to work rebranding my old business plan around this air steam trailer.

When I was about 5 my mother and father divorced, for about a year while my dad got back on his feet, we lived in a trailer. I went form riches to rags over night. I have no shame in that and I usually tend to embrace where I came from because it motivated me to become who I am. I was basically trailer trash, right? You bet, for those who didn't know me or my situation, that was how I was judged. I had a crazy idea to exaggerate trailer trash and we did just that. We were going to serve badass gourmet burgers out of a trailer but we were going to glam this bitch up! First of all, for those of you unfamiliar with the Airstream trailer, it is a Twinkie shaped camper, built of shinny stainless steel and in my opinion very, very "it" centric. I wanted to create a concept juxtaposed – meaning gourmet food out of a trailer. A shinny trashy trailer glammed up in a multi-million dollar urban living loft and retail park on par with something right out of Las Vegas. It doesn't get more opposite than that, but it worked. That was part one of our "it". Additionally, we wanted to have a high-end product in a low-end environment. Our purpose was to reject the establishment brands of the time that said you have to have a million dollar build out to be gourmet. We wanted to be the approachable gourmet who didn't take ourselves seriously but we took what we did very seriously. In fact our core purpose was 110% focus on the details or as we later would coin, "The devil is in the details."

Now, we weren't going to just serve an expensive gourmet burger, so how were we going to position our burger to be worth its price? And being sold out of a trailer? First, we needed to craft an amazing, one of a kind burger. So we reached out to a butcher we had worked with for years and we gave them our formula.

We decided that if we mixed 30% ground brisket with 30% beef short rib and 40% ground chuck we would get a perfect lean to fat ratio with no trim fat added and an amazing tasting burger to boot.

We went back and forth with the formula for a few weeks until it was the right grind consistency, flavor and the size we liked. We now had the beginning of our product that would align with our purpose. If you are a nerdy foodie or as I like to call it a "Food-tard" like me, that story might sound nice, but to most people it's a little wordy. So this is the "it" we crafted regarding our burgers.

"We use a local USDA choice blend of brisket, ground chuck & beef short rib ground fresh daily for "A Damn Good Burger" cooked on charcoal." ~ **Hella Burger**

How's that for "it"? We literally opened up the "it" can and painted our whole concept this exact same way. Here are some more examples of my "it" for this concept.

Do you remember the old shiny, corrugated, aluminum trash cans? The kind you see in cartoons with the alley cat? We bought those and they were spread around our picnic area with the words **TRAILER TRASH** stenciled on them with spray paint.

At Hella Burger the names of some of our burgers were the Rockabilly, Devil Went Down To Georgia, Trailer Trash, On the Lamb, Dance with the Devil, just to name a few.

None of our burgers were plain or lip service. The Devil Went Down to Georgia for example started with our "Damn Good Burger" peach marmalade, fried red onions, brie cheese and red vein heirloom spinach.

Our "On the Lamb" was local ground lamb with a cucumber, onion tomato salad with mint yogurt and a pickled mint, carrot & spinach slaw.

We also sold homemade "Devil's food cake Dingdongs" and "Homemade Angel food cake Twinkies". These are just a few menu items to give you the feel for our menu branding.

Here is just a bit more "it" relative to our concepts. We had a permanent 3 wire rope style fence (framed kind of like a boxing ring) around our pea gravel yard that was filled with red and orange picnic tables and yellow umbrellas (Hellish Colors). The top of the yard was covered with strewn carnival style Edison lights and we had big black paver stones that led up to the ordering window of the airstream. The black slate paver stones were inscribed in red with the words "Good Intentions" in a devilish font (As the path to the Hella was paved in good intentions).

We played devil and angel themed music exclusively on our playlist, like Hells Bells, Devil Went Down to Georgia, Take these broken wings, On the Arms of an Angel, Stairway to Heaven, Rob Zombie, etc.

We had a big catch iron tip bell labeled "Hell's Bells" that we would ring every time someone gave a tip.

We had secret marketing passwords like, "give me my Damn Fries!" and when you said so, you would get your fries for free (more about password marketing later).

While this may sound kitch, it was our "IT" and "IT"

worked very well. We were well before the movie Chef or the food truck craze and we did ours in a stationary airstream trailer.

We took our orders at the window on IPads with Square credit card technology (before anyone in the industry was using it). People always talked about us, we did tremendous sales and more importantly we were very profitable.

One last "it" to share before we move on. At this point I am starting to feel very self-indulgent, my apologies for that! When we placed our ads for employees it read something like this.

"Now hiring: "Gypsies" - passionate, creative food people to join our team of hell raisers. Tattoos and piercings are not mandatory but are greatly welcomed."

And guess what kind of people we got? The kind of people we wanted.

And guess what kind of customers we got? The kind of customers we wanted! The carnival atmosphere lovin, curious foodies. The hipsters, the techies, the industry Gypsies, the soccer moms who wanted to be the edgy, cool mom, the business guy who had to entertain a client with both dinner and a show… and the media. Yeah, it was a **"damn good plan"!**

Get "IT"?

and one that would have to be an online version do to how frequently FB changes their shit! – Grrrr!)

Next are the "pay per click" ads, "pop-up" ads and other "site advertising". Most of these are not usually as micro as Face Book in their depth of analytics (Google is getting close), meaning that they do not always hit the small geographical area you are intending. Some work but I don't spend a ton of time here because I don't see this as valuable as the categories proceeding this one. The internet is becoming more drilled down and more capable of measuring where people are located geographically. With new technologies like Google Plus and location services, this will come full circle in no time at all. In the months and years to come all internet searches will be filtered by your IP address to recognize your specific location and give you the results of your query based solely upon your geographic location. But again, doing it yourself is a little more complicated than I can invest in right now and the change is much too rapid for a book in print to ever hope to keep up with. I will likely write an advanced follow up book on this subject matter alone and host it online.

That said, another form of internet marketing is also your website. The reason I don't really call that marketing is because most restaurateurs don't really use their website as a marketing tool but instead as an information page.

NOTE: If you do not (for some crazy reason) have a website right now, check out GoDaddy.com or Wix.com right now! Here you can build your own website for free. It is easy and it doesn't require any coding or graphic artist skillset. It may not be everything you want but something is better than nothing!

There are a few free and useful ways to drive new traffic to your website like Google Places now called Google Plus Local and Google Maps but outside of that, I will cover your website when we get to internal marketing. I am not going to go in depth on Google Places because now that you are aware of it (if your weren't already) you can... Google it! or YouTube how to set up your Google Plus Local.

NOTE: When setting up your Google+Local page add as much info, pictures, hours of operations, videos, etc. as the site will allow. Also, a word to the wise, Google has a distinct way of setting up addresses. It will change the format of your address after you enter it to read the Google way. If the format is different than the way you have your address on your website, change the format on your website to match the Google format. This will drive more traffic to your website and give your website more hits thus moving it up in the search engine results listing. You always want your website to be the first thing to come up in a search engine result of your name. The reason being, you want to be at the top because that is most commonly the option picked. If the first result in the search engine is your website you control the message as opposed to a peer review site like Yelp controlling the message instead.

Here are a few things we have had great success with on our Web Page.

ONLINE STORE:

We sell merchandise, cook-books, sauces, catering, clothing, gift certificates and more... on-line! We also have free recipes and videos with cooking techniques, instructions and cool tips for entertaining. We have a shopping cart and we do a tremendous business on-line.

FREE $10 Gift Cards

We use a "Pop Up" ad on our site when someone visits our page. Quite simply, when they go to exit the page, a window pops up and says,

> **"Hey… if you're coming to see us tonight… we'd like to treat you. Here's $10. Type in your info here and we'll send you a $10 gift card right now."**

Backstory to that one: They may or may not have been coming to our restaurant tonight. Likely they were just looking at us and a few other concepts. So to win their favor and be the one they pick, we bribe them.

We get their email address, name, birthday and zip code. We take that data and see who is visiting our page and what percentage of those emailed took us up on our offer (we can count how many auto-responder emails went out and how were cashes in). Not only did we see a large number of these return, we turn it off on Friday and Saturday nights (we don't need to discount our busy time). It is just a promotional tool that we use during our slower nights.

In addition to the direct call to action (The gift card is only valid that night and it says so right on the print out) we also get their important demographic info along with an email address. We sign them up for our birthday program where we email them a gift for their birthday and we also send them a few other call to action emails throughout the year.

These are just a few ideas we have had great success with on our website that you can use to wet your whistle.

NOTE: *Website Etiquette*
- *Make sure you have a printable menu on your website. It should be a PDF simple, black and white menu (heavily colored backgrounds take a ton of ink).*
- *Make sure your address & phone number are on every page.*
- *Make sure your webpage is up to date and that it reflect the brand image in a good way.*
- *Avoid clutter!*
- *If you are going to post an offer, have a call to action.*
- *Have a way together peoples information in exchange for your call to action.*
- *Don't be cheap here, have a great website.*

Look at some of the cool stuff Chipotle does if you want a reference for a great website. (Youtube the Scarecrow video)

So, that's it? That's internet marketing? No! That's what internet marketing is to me for how as it applies to this book and its message (in a vacuum). I do not want to send you down a path that will take up all of your time and study. The ideas in this book will have some internet related channels but I will have to leave it at that because I don't want you to spend a ton of time and study to implement things outside of your scope. I want you to experience workable, money making, marketing ideas with amazing and quick impacts… the quickest way possible.

SOCIAL MEDIA MARKETING

Some facts before we get started.

- **Over 50% of the population today is under 30 years of age.**

- **Over 96% of Millennials belong to a social media platform.**

- **Social Media has overtaken porn as the number one activity on the web.**

- **It took radio over 38 years to reach an audience of 50 million people, television took 13 years, the internet took 4 years and Facebook hit over 200 million in less than one year.**

- **78% of consumers trust peer recommendations vs. the 13% that trust advertisement recommendations.**

(Source: socialnomics.com)

The statistics and this category can keep going for miles and miles. These are the channels I use for different ideas on the internet but they are not specifically internet market ideas as "internet marketing is defined".

I count Social Media different than internet marketing and I break Social Media into two types that we will dive into below. Some of these applications apply in both categories so I am breaking them into the categories by the way that I use them for marketing purposes.

> **NOTE:** *Certain demographics seem to have more popular types of Social Media that can vary by region, age and demographics but the following are no doubt the kings of all categories...*

Social Media: Peer to Peer
- Facebook *(this one has a dual purpose)*
- YouTube *(could also be considered a search engine)*
- Twitter
- LinkedIn
- Pinterest
- Instagram
- Snapchat
- Vine

Social Media: Peer Review
- Facebook *(this one has a dual purpose)*
- Yelp
- Urban Spoon
- Trip Advisor
- Zagat

This is enough of a list for an entire division of one company to manage so let's try to focus on these and only be mindful of the rest. In the next chapter I will discuss ideas on how to market in these channels so please don't be worried that I am not diving in to all of them right now. I just want to focus on all of the free places you can get your message out to your audience when it comes to creating a marketing campaign. If you remember to go back to these sites when you put your offer together, you will find a good offer can fit in just about all of these sites.

GRASSROOTS MARKETING

This is the type of marketing that is usually more community focused. Ways to do grass roots marketing would include putting a program together for schools. One of my favorites is "Back to School Night".

Quick Idea: Go to your neighborhood school before the beginning of the year and help them with a back to school night. Create a "Meet the principal" event and create enough flyers or vouchers for each student to take home to mom and dad. Make the flyer a $5 gift card (not a $5 off). Or offer a kids eat free night or something like that on the flyer. Also, offer to give 10% of all **profits** to the school.

Note: I said 10% of the profits. You can choose any amount you want but be careful to use the word profits not proceeds. The implication is much different so please pay attention to your wording.

Other types of grassroots campaigns would be things like holding a toy drive or a fund raiser or a charity event.

NOTE: Charity is one thing I am more passionate about than nearly anything. But that doesn't mean I just find any charity to donate my time, money and resources to. I find divisions of proven, legitimate, local charities that are inline with my purpose.. The more local the charity, the more impactful it can be for your business. Don't just choose Breast Cancer; find a local Breast Cancer division. It will affect more people locally which is where your money will go and where your revenue will come from. Another belief of mine, relative to charity, is that I will only help those that help themselves. I am of the "hand up" mentality vs. the "hand out" mentality. That is just my personally philosophy but I share it because I love success stories and they are harder to find when they are the later instead of the former.

EVEN MORE GRASSROOTS PROGRAMS...

- **Industry Events**
- **Local Businesses**
- **Joint Ventures**
- **Your Neighbors**

QUICK IDEA: Here is another quick idea on JV's (joint ventures) and working with retail neighbors. For one client I was working with, we were looking for a good local partner to share our customers with and vice versa. I love dry cleaners because only people with disposable income get their cloths dry cleaned, they also understand quality and we love people who have those two traits. So, we went to the neighboring dry cleaner and proposed an idea. We would share a discount in-store from them and they would hang a "Hanging Offer" on each order they sent out. The place I was working with was a gourmet pizza concept. What goes better with red sauce than dry cleaning? What gets a dry cleaner more cloths faster than red sauce? See the marriage? It worked out really well. The offer was my standard $10 cut out, gift card... you guessed it, "no strings attached".

ANOTHER QUICK IDEA: We also tapped in to another market quite by accident. When I was buying a car one time, the salesman could tell I was really thinking hard about this deal. He said, do me a favor, why don't you and your wife take the car, go grab some lunch on me and talk it over. He then gave us the keys to the car we were looking at and a $10 gift card to a local restaurant right around the corner. We took him up on the lunch and later bought the car.

When I went back to work, I started printing $10 gift certificates and I took them to the car dealership the next day. I spoke to the GM and pitched the idea (like it was my own) and he loved it. He didn't have to pay anything for the gift cards. I was giving him free food and a free (bad ass) idea to build loyalty and authenticity with his customers. At that point he had asked me if we delivered. I said we do large catering but not small orders. He then asked if we would be willing to deliver a standing order every Saturday. He explained that Saturday's were their busiest day and all of their employees usually worked and he liked to buy them lunch as a thank you for their hard work and also so they didn't have to leave. And boom goes the dynamite! One hand washes the other. We later ended up doing their monthly inventory dinner delivered as well. Oh and of course we reached out to every dealership in the area to get the same thing going and boy did it print. The Saturday thing was particularly awesome because our lunch business was pretty soft on Saturdays.

INDUSTRY MARKETING

I know I already covered industry events but industry marketing is different. These are the people who work in your market.

If you don't already have a SIN event, start one. SIN is short for "Service Industry Night". The best thing about the people in our business is they love to drink and understand the value of quality and service! They also usually have cash in hand, another trait I love in customers! One of the first General Management jobs I had was in La Jolla, CA. I worked for a locally owned concept for the guy who was an early mentor to me in this industry. We had a pretty sweet gig we worked out together. He would work days and I would work nights. He was older and our lunch crowd was an older residential crowd in the area. This was a perfect match for him. I would work nights when our business was largely younger people and tourists and families with kids and industry people during the late night... more my crowd.

We had a manager who would float for us on our days off and double down with one of us during heavy volume shifts. Theft behind the bar was a common point of pain for both of us and we worked to ensure we minimized theft. We also knew a big part of our audience was the service industry. We were the only bar and grill in the area opened until 2:00 am. Most of the other restaurants closed in our neighborhood between 10:00 pm and midnight. Thus, the service industry folks came to have their after work cocktails with us. We played with a bunch of ideas so that our bartenders could give free drinks but no matter how we painted the picture, it always led to creative liberty. Basically, if you give people permission to pour free drinks they can rationalize doing it whenever they see fit and we couldn't have that. So I decided to start making a SIN shot for every night of the week. We didn't have to but we wanted to. This would give us control over what our bartenders would be giving away and still give the hook up to our peeps!

I would take any of the free samples or bonus bottle program alcohol we would get from our vendors and make some kind of unique shot. I would make sure the cost was minimal and controlled. When the shots were out, so too were the free drinks. We made our SIN folks aware it was first come first serve and this created what is called a…"Call to Action".

- In the marketing world a "call to action" is basically what makes people make decisions quickly or they lose out.

We didn't want the SIN folks even thinking about where to go for a drink after work. We did have some competition in this venue but we knew if we got them first, they would stay till the end. We did require that our service professionals either came in their uniforms or with a current paystub (and ID of course). We thought we had already had a pretty good SIN crowd but after the free shot program, we doubled our crowd after 11:00 pm. and they nearly always stayed until close. What's more, the walk in traffic was busier too. People love to go where the people are and service industry people are a great magnet for drawing new business because they are usually young, hip and attractive with pretty good personalities.

WARNING: *SIN folks are also known to be a little rowdy.* *Be extra mindful not to over serve, keep them happy but* *under control and always be respectful.*

Another SIN story that worked out in quite a different way happened when I first started working with the guy I mentioned earlier named Mark. Mark had a Coal-fired VPN Pizzeria concept. First of its kind in the market place and authentic as hell. This guy had me tell him who all of the players were in the market and then he spent all of his start up time eating around at different high end restaurants and chatting up the best chefs, GM's, Bartenders and owners in town. He would patronize their business and introduce his amazing food concept and quality ideals to these people. He would massage their ego and let them know how import their feedback was to him because he loved the way they did their thing and it would mean the world to have them come try his food for free just for the honest feedback. He supported their causes, their beliefs and he was non-threatening because he was a pizza concept.

What came from this strategy was a crowd of loyal chefs and industry followers that would not only migrate to his place often but they would tell their friends, their customers and their family about this amazing place and how they had to go try it. This is one of the most brilliant and tactical industry marketing strategies I have even seen.

Guest Chef Night! Say no more. This is a strategy we would employ all the time. We would pay some of the best local chefs in the area that did noncompeting products and have them come apply their craft and interpretation to our concept type of food.

These guys were also our buddies or became our buddies and the events helped put us on the map. For those that got it, we didn't even pay them. We ended up doing the same in exchange for one of their events, or charities or a time when they were just simply in need. We didn't mean to create community that was just the beautiful byproduct of the mindset. It was one part local celebrity endorsement, one part creative cooking and one part bringing the best chefs best customers to our restaurant. Great chefs have a great following of supporters that are always interested in the exciting things their chefs are doing and these followers love to see these chefs in a different venue with a different canvass. This is an amazing idea and I encourage anyone to try it! It also creates an amazing industry community that makes it a better industry in any market place.

INTERNAL MARKETING

This is seemingly a no brainer but it doesn't happen enough. It is amazing how many people rely on Facebook to let their current customers know what is going on in their restaurants yet they post nothing in their restaurants to draw them back.

Here are a handful of ideas on how to market to your internal customers to get them back faster. These same ideas apply to all marketing but experimenting internally is a great way to practice your ideas on the people who already love you.

• THE BOUNCE BACK

A bounce back is a classic way to get people back with a "call to action" also called in the industry a "CTA". Here is a classic example of a bounce back. When you go to Starbucks to get a coffee in the morning, they offer you a half price drink that same day if you come back after 3:00. I choose to do things a little more unique. Here are a few of the bounce back ideas I have used.

I always empower my servers to buy a new customer a drink on their next visit. Basically, my staff always used frequency questions when waiting on a customer they had not waited on before. Quite simply at the greeting they would say to our guest, "You've been here before right?" If the guess answered no, we would walk them through what was great on the menu and what we were known for. At the end of the meal, the server was allowed to put a free drink card in the book that said, thanks for dining with me tonight. Next time you come in, ask for me and I would love to buy you your first drink. The server would then put their name on the card. This promoted our guests to get a favorite server each time they came and the servers, who got it, loved it because they were always the busiest servers.

We had a literal "bounce back" promotion we did in October where we would take a pink racquet ball that was worth $10. Anytime a guest would donate to our local Breast Cancer Aware Charity, we would give that guest a bounce back ball. The $10 pink ball would say from "that guest's name" (written in black sharpie and dated by our staff) and would also say "worth $10 bucks". That guest could give that ball to anyone they liked and if the ball was returned, the person returning it would get $10 off their food or drink and we would also donate an addition $10 to the charity in the original guests name. This was a wildly successful bounce back promotion that was fun and for a great cause!

• LIMITED TIME OFFER

AKA the "LTO". You are probably aware of the "LTO" idea in its simplest form. It happens daily in restaurants all around the world. Fresh whole Maine lobster is a classic example. If you don't get there early, they run out. In the BBQ industry the secret "LTO" is usually the burnt ends. These are things that customers love and they are in limited supply. I work with an amazing Mexican Concept out of Los Angeles that has a green corn tamale that might be one of the best things you have ever put in your mouth. They are called El Cholo (so you can go try them). They only run these for a certain time of the year and when the season starts, people go crazy! There are tons of great food items out there that are simply only available seasonally like specialty produce, soft shell crabs, fresh Halibut, etc. If you are not building hype around your menu with items like this before they come and before they go, you are missing a great marketing opportunity!

Other companies have even captured the success of these items on a larger corporate scale. McDonald's has the McRib and the Shamrock Shake. They push these items during their slower times of the year to create a sales boost. One of my favorite chefs in the world hates McDonalds but will always head there when the McRib comes out.

• REFERRAL PROGRAMS

We often did referral programs with Hotels and the concierge staff. The concept was really simple. We would do a two way promotion. If a hotel employee sent a guest our way, the guest would get something for free when they told us which hotel and which employee sent them and the employee would get a $10 visa gift card for every group they sent. We would have cards with our Restaurant logo, an offer (like free appetizer) and a space for the hotel employee to enter their name and hotel name. The employee was instructed to come in and pick up their money on the last day of the period (which for us was always on the last Sunday of the month). Sunday was historically our slowest day of the week and majority of those folks that came in to pick up their gift cards would hang out for some food or a drink. Not too bad, huh?

We did a similar deal with a car dealerships in a story I mentioned earlier.

• WALL ST. URINAL

What's going on in your restaurant or bar? How do people know? Some of the best marketing space in a restaurant is in the bathroom. Create a really simple, informative message and put it in the bathrooms. Make it easy and quick to read. I use to work at a concept that literally had the newspaper in a framed box above the urinal called the

"Wall St. Urinal". That is great to keep the guest occupied and interject some humor but take it a step further and put up the things that are happening in your restaurant. Don't stop at the urinal. Put it on the doors on the bathroom stall interior. There is nothing to look at in there but your phone and that is gross. Change the content often, frame the message in a nice presentation box and keep it updated.

I hate table tents because I think they are cheap looking and they hardly get viewed but putting an upcoming event on a nice glossy card in the guest check book is a nice marketing touch. Again, don't flood the message with tons of info. Have a two sentence pitch that makes it interesting and gives them dates, price and details of the event.

In certain environments, I am also big on hanging eye catching media form the ceilings if it matches your look and atmosphere. The sign doesn't have to say anything and it doesn't even have to be a sign. It can be an object or a widget that ties to the idea and makes people ask.

Example: We use to hang decorative Picnic Baskets from the ceiling in a deli concept I worked with. To help build our lunch business we launched a picnic concept. We were located across the street from a heavily toured park, great for families and dates alike. We also had the picnic baskets set up in the retail space but the ceiling hangers got more attention than the retail facing of the item and it led customers to ask about them.

Get outside of the box, by marketing inside of your box!

• STAFF PITCH

Have the staff pitch the guests on what is up and coming. If you are having a live band or a big event or even launching a picnic basket, have the staff ask the guests if they love live music or ever do a picnic in the park? If they do, you have them tell the guest about what is up coming. Maybe even give them a flyer or nice glossy publication style postcard. It can be anything for any type of event or marketing idea, but get the staff excited and engaged and have them do the promoting for you. Have an offer; make sure the guest knows what is in it for them, aside from just the event. Maybe complimentary beer or wine tastings for the first 100 people... something like that, you dig?

• MENU MENTIONS

If they fit your brand, make sure you post upcoming events inside of your most viewed marketing tool. Put a little flyer in the menu promoting upcoming events, new menu launch dates, wine dinners, etc. You can keep a mention short just by listing the event and directing your guests to "ask your server for more details" or "check us out on Facebook/Our website for more deets".

• TABLE TENTS

So, I am not a big fan of these, like I said before, but in the appropriate vehicle these can be effective. I think the acrylic table tents look cheap and get filthy, chipped and often have the liquor of choice shamelessly promoting their product instead of yours. With nice triangle style, repurposed style or industry flip board style table information holders that reflect your brand appropriately, these can be a great source of information for your guests. Just keep the message clean, simple and to the point.

People get so exhausted just looking at a paragraph written on a page that they usually don't bother to read it. Less is more in your marketing offers.

NOTE: When it comes to sponsoring alcohol or food brands or anything like that, within your restaurant, on a menu, on a glass, in the bathroom, etc. I rarely allow other brands to market within my units unless it is on the bottle of alcohol itself. The only exception I make to this is when the brand value is equal to or greater than mine or complimentary to us or what we are marketing at that time. That includes some alcohol brands but it needs to be complimentary. People will tune out when they are getting confusing messages all over the place. You also run the risk of looking like a messy, brand, sell out! The interior of your concept is your precious space and needs to be coveted the most!

• FREQUENCY CARDS

This is a really effective strategy for many concepts. At Hella Burger we did a loyalty card that had a buildup to the end. Unlike most frequency programs we offered something free on just about every visit. The first time signing up for a card we got their email (more about building an email list later). They also got a punch which was worth $5. The second time they got free parmesan garlic fries. The 3rd time they received a free drink. The 4th time they got nothing but the 5th time they got free fries and a drink. The 5th time they got another $5 and the 6th and 7th time was nothing because on the 8th time they got

$15. That was our PPA and we thought is reasonable to give them a free meal on their 8th visit worth the value of our average PPA. We ran these once per quarter with an expiration date. Our card was called "The Devil's Advocate". We saw better returns than I have ever seen with a buy 9 get the 10th free. This was a more manageable program to the customer and created a faster return because it was incrementally driven with a big payoff at the end.

We even offered to keep them in a file box for our customers. The deal is, I wanted to make it as convenient and rewarding as possible for my guests to get "the hook up". Plus, when the card was in the box with their name, we had the most valuable tool in the world. In a psychology study done years ago it showed that any person's favorite word is their name. We wanted to use that as often as we could. The card idea seems to work best in a quick service concept but try to rework this idea anyway you see fit in your concept. Just make sure it doesn't cheapen your brand image.

• DATE NIGHT

During our slow days we created a co-sponsored program with a babysitting service that was reputable and local. We met with the service and pitched them the idea. We will drive new business to your service on your slow nights and create a bunch of new customers for you by promoting your place during our "Date Night" marketing push. We encouraged the babysitting service to give us a screaming deal that we could pass on to our customers for this promotion and we all win.

- And the deal went something like this...

IMPRESS YOUR WIFE!
You both deserve a break!

- **Tuesday night is date night!**
- **DINNER FOR 2: choice of appetizer, soup or salad and 2 entrees for $50 bucks!**

- **Complimentary Wine tastings hosted by Cake Bread Cellars.**

- <u>**Plus we'll help you with the child care too.**</u>

Nanny's on Call Drop-in child care has partnered with us to give you $20 off your first visit. Right around the corner from the restaurant.

Make your reservations early; we usually book up a week in advance. We'll book the nanny for you.

• FISHING FOR BUSINESS

The fish bowl reimagined! This is an idea from the old days but the concept is still solid.

Back in the day we use to raffle off free offers when a guest dropped their business card in our fish bowl. This idea is used to build business however you want. If you are a busy lunch spot, offer a dinner for 2. If you are busy for dinner do the opposite. The same would work for Happy Hour. We did this in many forms. We had one of our raffle drops in a big huge martini glass and we offered a free happy hour party for you and 10 friends. This was to build our happy hour business and we did it weekly. The offer was one free drink per person and free small plates to feed 10.

Here is the genius! We pulled every single card and wouldn't you know it… they were all winners. We had one grand prize winner and all of the other cards would be notified similar to the example that follows.

We would either call them on the phone around 3:00 pm or send them an email at the same time and the conversation went like this.

EMAIL
Dear (Whomever),

CONGRATUALTIONS (their name)! YOU WON!

This is so and so from such and such. I am the "position" and I wanted to personally thank you for being a great customer. We wanted to let you know, that while you didn't win our grand prize for our "Be Social" contest, you were our runner up.

Please bring in up to 5 of your friends for 1 free drink each and 5 free appetizers. Just bring in this email and show it to us. The offer expires in 30 days so grab some friends and come hang with us. Thanks for dropping your cards in our "Be Social" contest.

Sincerely,
Your name (Include a digital, colorized signature)
Email
Phone Number
Link to website

NOTE: *If you noticed, they were the runner up winner. Just to clear the air, everyone who didn't win was a runner up. Hence, everyone won! Additionally, before giving away alcohol please check your local laws and ordinances.*

If time permitted, I would always prefer to call. It helped to make a more genuine connection and the return on the offer was always higher. I would still send them a certificate for the prize via email.

As the years have moved forward I have reimagined these same ideas but I have repurposed them to fit more modern technology. Now instead of the fishbowl, I use a system called an auto responder. The guest is prompted to text their name and email to a phone number for a random drawing for the same types of prizes.

Again, we collect all of the data and the auto responder thanks them automatically in a text message that we pre-write. The only difference is I usually reward a guest right away with a $5 digital gift card in that response text so that they can use it right then and there on the spot. All they have to do is show the auto responder text and date to the person serving them and they get their $5 gift card as a **BONUS thank you** prize for entering.

The reason I employ this tactic now is because the service will do everything for me. It will capture the person's name, phone number and email into a direct database. It will also respond right away so I don't have to do it individually later. The program will even do the drawing and send out all of the emails that I have already prewritten. It's that easy.

Either way, whether you go old school or new, this one works unbelievably well and I also end up having a great list to go back to when I am going to announce something else that is going on in the future.

These are just a few of the ideas we have put in place with great response and tremendous results. Now that you know all of these different industry terms for types of marketing, Google them and see tons of other great ideas that you can draw from and start using right away! You do not have to copy them exact and of course, make sure that the offer lines up with your brand.

STUPID SHIT WORKS

"Talk sense to a fool and he calls you foolish." ### *~ Euripides*

I know stupid shit works because I always measure my results and when you are forced to look back at your success you will usually come to the same conclusion I do.

- "Wow, that was easy. It was so easy in fact it was stupid."

This is what I find when I study what worked. Unfortunately the same is true of my failures. The point being, if you do nothing expect nothing. However, when you do something anything can happen. The lesson is… **DO SOMETHING!**

So here is a list of stupid shit I have done both in my concepts and in the concepts of my clients.

While the following ideas may seem simple, crude and even crazy, remember this. "A confused mind does nothing". And of course the KISS principle. **K**eep **I**t **S**imple **S**tupid.

PAID SIGN HOLDERS

I have paid and fed a homeless guy to hold a sign that used to say will work for food and then had him change his sign to…

"I'm not hungry! Joe's fed me and they will feed you too! Plus they pay me to hold this sign!" "God Bless" EAT AT JOES!

People loved the fact that we were feeding a guy already standing there and paying him too. It did really well.

GAMBLE FOR THE CHECK

At the launch of a new menu I had signs posted in the restaurant for a month promoting the "New Menu Launch" date. Here is a graphic of what was hanging in the restaurant.

Tuesday February 3rd

On Tuesday, February 3rd. Play rock, paper, scissors with your cashier to win your lunch!

This effort was an event for a deli and it had an effect of nearly 4x the average lunch time sales. We did it on a Tuesday because it was historically the slowest day of the week.

Another variation of **"gambling for the check"** can work the exact same way but instead of rock, paper, scissors, you can flip a coin instead. This is a great way to boost a new happy hour launch or build traffic on Facebook with this offer on a slow night. We would often allow our bartenders a chance to do this on a slower evening. They would promote it on Facebook with their personal friends and clients and we would promote it on our FB Fan Page.

FLIP A COIN FOR ½ OFF

For a new menu launch (at a Mexican concept I was working with) we decided to do a promotion where people could come in on day two of the menu launch (day one required us working out any bugs and making sure day two was set up for success). Each server had a Mexican coin in their pocket and at the end of the meal they would play "Heads or Tails" with the guest for 50% off of their bill.

We had signs promoting it throughout the restaurant for two weeks. We posted pictures and some great artwork and copy writing done for our social media and the website.

We also started a preview menu that showcased a few of the items in advance (to both promote the new menu and get the staff comfortable with the new feel). Knowing we were changing, cutting and adding so many new items, we wanted to get in front of the potential backlash (similar to the Del Rosso's story) so we created some great hype.

A TRIP TO MEXICO

For the same Mexican concept above, we also ran a tandem event tied to this new menu launch. For any guest who ordered one of the new items during the two week pre-launch period, they would get their name entered into a drawing. On third day of the new menu launch we had live music and crazy drinks specials launching our new drink menu as well. When they came in on that night, we did the drawing for the trip for two to Mexico. The only rule was they had to be present to win.

Both events drew a ton of fan fare and helped ensure the re-launch was a great success.

STAFF

To tie into the staff section above, we also did a lot of marketing with an empowered staff. To take a page out of the Ritz Carlton, our staff was given freedom to do whatever it takes to make a guest happy. Each member of our staff was given a business card. They were allowed to pick a title for their job that related to their job and their personality. One bartender we of ours came up with the best title to date called the **"Head Intoxicologist"**. Our staff was also allowed to buy drinks, comp meals and take care of any other guest needs they deemed appropriate. We would often review the effect and try to measure it. It is amazing how an empowered staff will do exactly the opposite with discretionary spending when they are allowed to do it. Again, the process requires review and group discussion. Sometimes there were things we didn't approve of but more times than not, we found great new ideas in this approach.

PASSWORD MARKETING

During our slow days we started a Facebook marketing campaign built around password marketing. Mondays and Tuesday we would alternate our offer with a password good for that day only.

We did this every Monday and Tuesday for three months and there were too many to name but here is an example of one.

At our Hella Burger Concept we would offer free stuff with a password.

On Facebook we would post a picture of our Garlic Parmesan Fries with a caption that would say...

Just say "Give Me My Damn Fries" with the purchase of any gourmet burger and get your fries for free today!

We could measure how many we did every time we got the password. We would track our total number of customers for the day vs. our historical daily average and measure the results. Some worked better than other but we never saw less than a 20% increase over our average daily head count and sales.

YELP OFFERS

On our Yelp page we always had a free offer. It was

password based once again. The passwords we would do for any particular thing was always different from Facebook to Yelp or printed advertising. That way we could always measure where it was coming from and how impactful it was.

WEBSITE MARKETING

Recently I developed what is called an "exit pop" for one of our clients. An "exit pop" is a pop up message attached to your webpage. When you go to exit the page or go back, the "pop up" message comes up with an offer or greeting. While in many applications these are annoying, we framed it in a really simple way. The exit pop looks exactly like a gift card and said… "Thank you for checking us out. Type in your email address and we'll send you a free $10 gift card. No strings attached."

The email address is critical for future marketing campaigns. Since this is the first time we offered this we are still in beta so the results are a bit premature. As of right now, it is tracking very well and the client is seeing many of the gift cards being returned.

PUBLISH A COOK BOOK FOR FREE!

Write and publish a cook book. This is literally one of the easiest things you can do. I have done this a number of times and the execution is easy. First go to the inter-webs and download a free cook book template. Then, simply go to Amazon's create space and upload your book once you have filled in the template. It can be, but doesn't have to be, current menu items. It can be a dumbed down version of things you currently do, have done in the past, have run as specials or for caterings, etc. The cost per book in black and white is a few bucks and if you want to add color pictures that will run close to about $10. At the end of the day, "Create Space" will publish it through amazon, help you create a free cover and have it queued up ready to print on the spot.

This is an excellent marketing vehicle because you do not have to order 100 copies and have the inventory on hand and be out the cash. You can feature the cook book on your website with a link to Amazon where your loyal followers can order it. Most importantly, buy your own copies and have them in your store. More on that in a minute.

What is also great about doing the cook book is they are all "print on demand" so they do not print and ship until they have been ordered and paid for. It is of no cost to you any time they are ordered and you set your own price. After you cover the cost for amazon to print them, the rest of the money is pure profit that goes right in to your bank account.

Now, regarding the in store cook books. First thing you do when the cook book is ready, is you order about 50 copies. The cost to you, the author, is the cost to print. Like I said, just a few bucks. Then you start advertising around the store and the internet and Facebook that you are going to be having a Cookbook release party at the restaurant. Build the hype and you can even do a book signing party at the same time. Display a nice retail stand in the front of the store and make it print baby!

Make sure to always leave the book out and visible so the "walker-buy" can see it. Think of all the street cred that brings to your business when they see you have a published cookbook up front or in the window and on your website. At Danny Meyer's restaurants in New York he has the copies of his bestselling book **"Setting the Table"** and **"Second Helpings"** everywhere, including displayed on the bar and at the host stand.

Another great thing about this process is that you can edit the book or pull it from Amazon at any time at no cost. When that works and you see the impact, do another and another and so on. It is limitless! This is one my favorite and simplest ideas. Now for the bonus, you just created a brand new revenue stream in your restaurant. It called retail baby! Think about what else you can sell in your restaurant for $20 that cost you around $2 to make. This idea is worth the cost of this book alone! Good luck. GO DO IT!

<u>YOUTUBE IDEA</u>

This part of marketing has gotten so simple, as of late, that if you have an IPhone (or any camera phone for that matter) this is a no brainer. When you take a video with an IPhone today it prompts you to load it to YouTube when you complete the video. It's that simple. Create your own YouTube channel first. Here is what you do with this amazing technology.

Do a cooking demo for simple family meal ideas.
- Show them how to prepare for a big party at home.
- Show them how to make something homemade like

marshmallows, the perfect pancake, signature dressings, crème brulee, etc.

Show them how to make some killer party drinks!

- Offer your favorite cocktail recipes.
- Show them some mixology techniques.

Make sure to plug your restaurant all over the place and when loading the video make sure to use as many keywords in the description as possible.

And here's the bonus gift. Every time you load a video you increase the visibility of your website. You see, years ago your website location on a search engine result was driven by how many people viewed your page and how many key words you had and if you paid for that positioning. Today YouTube searches not only moves your video up in rank but it moves your restaurant website and Facebook pages up in rank on the web as well (that is of course providing you put your restaurants name as one of the key words embedded in your video). Don't worry if you don't know how to do this. When you upload your video, it prompts you right then and there to enter in your key words. If you are still intimidated by this, ask one of your young employees and they will show you.

STOP AT THE START

"People usually stop at the start"
~ Unknown

I have heard this quote my whole life and I don't know where it comes from but I know how true it is. Like anything inspiring or motivating, these things give birth to great new ideas. I have been consulting with restaurants for nearly two decades and I know this quote to be true because of what I see. It frustrates me so much that I made it a sociology study. While I am merely an amateur sociologist I believe my conclusion is solid. People usually don't start because something is either too complicated, too hard or the idea does not come with instructions. There is nothing worse than giving someone something you know will change their life and they do nothing with it.

Whether I charge for the consultation or I'm just giving someone advice, it still drives me crazy when people don't even try. What makes it worse is when I hear them bitch about their problems later. I know so truly and deeply that these ideas work and they will work for you that I will leave you with no excuses. And that is what this chapter is.

This chapter is a step by step review of how to get this done. It's kind of like that old saying "If you fish for a man he will eat for a day, if you teach a man to fish he will eat for a lifetime."

EXERCISE 5. – Getting it done!

1.) Know who you are.
    a. If you don't know who you are (as a brand) ask people. You may not like what you hear but at least you will know what to change.

2.) Capture the essence of your brand in two sentences or less.
    a. Anything is likely better than what you have now.
    b. Keep refining it.

3.) Know who your audience is.
    a. If you don't know, ask them. What they like to do, what they do for a living, favorite music, etc. Be interested and be interesting.
    b. Above all else… LISTEN!

4.) Create your USP/ESP or what I call the ASP!
    a. Study your competition
    b. Study the big brands
    c. Use a peer group.
    d. Have a contest on Facebook for a prize!

5.) Where do your peeps get their marketing?
    a. Find out where they get marketing info and start with those types of platforms for your campaigns.
    b. If you don't know… ASK!

6.) Create a list of great ideas.
    a. Write them all down

    b. Consult with a peer group

    c. Narrow it down to 3 at a time

    d. Roll them out and track their return

    e. Wash, Rinse and Repeat!

7.) If at first you don't succeed…

    a. Try, Try again

    b. Study the failure

    c. Tweak and try again

8.) Be remarkable!

    a. Always

    b. Always

    c. Always

9.) If you don't know how to do something

    a. Google it

    b. Check YouTube

    c. Talk to your staff!

10.) Forecast your ROI

    a. How much will it cost?

    b. How much will it return?

    c. Does it make sense?

BUILD A MARKETING CALENDAR

After you narrow down your ideas figure out how long they should run. Run them for a month, a quarter and/or indefinitely. I use a rule of three at a time and I try to make them fit based on the most relevant time of the year. Here is an example of one of my previous marketing calendars.

Marketing Calendar at a Glance		
JANUARY	**FEBRUARY**	**MARCH**
ROCK, PAPER, SCISSORS	VALENTINE'S DAY	MARCH MADNESS
YOUTUBE LESSONS	GAME NIGHT	GUEST CHEF PROGRAM
BOWL GAMES	SUPER BOWL	MARDI GRAS
NEW YEARS HANG OVER PARTY	GROUNDHOG DAY	ST. PATTY'S DAY
APRIL	**MAY**	**JUNE**
TAX BREAK	CINCO de MAYO	FATHER'S DAY PROMO
PARKING TICKET	ARMED FORCED DAY	GOLF PROMO
NEW MENU	PASSWORD MARKETING	SUMMER SOLITCE
EASTER BRUNCH	MOTHERS DAY	SUMMER NIGHTS
JULY	**AUGUST**	**SEPTEMBER**
RED, WHITE & BLUE PARTY	BACK TO SCHOOL NIGHT	KIDS NIGHT
BIRTHDAY BASH	COIN FLIP MONDAYS	LABOR DAY BASH
PARENT'S DAY - Date Night	END OF SUMMER PARTY	GRANDPARENTS DAY
PASSWORD MARKETING	BATTLE OF THE BANDS	FOOTBALL PARTY
OCTOBER	**NOVEMBER**	**DECEMBER**
NEW MENU	HOLIDAY PARTY PROMO	CHRISTMAS DAY PARTY
HARVEST PARTY	GIFT CARD PROMO	HOMELESS DINNER
BREAST CANCER BOUNCE BACK	VETRANS DAY	BIG ASS WINE DINNER
HALLOWEEN/DAYLIGHT SAVINGS	TOYS FOR TOTS	WORST HOLIDAY SWEATER PARTY

Look at October for an example. I did the "Pink Ball" for a bounce back promotion during October for Breast Cancer Awareness Month. I wanted to use a ball for my bounce back but not just any old ball. I was at my gym in October a year before when I saw the pink racquet balls and I built the idea around that.

If you live in every town USA you have a local furniture store. Have you ever noticed how the furniture store has a sale every month for no real furniture related reason?

Labor Day, Memorial Day, Arbor Day (Really?) Isn't furniture made out of trees?), President's Day, Fourth of July (because nothing says Freedom like buying a new couch!), the 10th Annual Easter Sale… You get the drift.

You likely haven't even thought about this before. You just get all excited and think you need to get some new shit because the deals are so amazing. Yet these deals seem to come up every single month. Hmmm.

Car dealers are the same way. Any excuse for marketing is a good excuse. Pick some ideas and get them on the calendar.

PLAN FOR THE CAMPAIGN

Dig in. Don't just run a program without having all of the above outlined steps dialed in.

- What do you have to do before you launch it?

- When will the printer have your materials back?

- How can your vendors, friends, family and staff help?

- Do you have the appropriate staff scheduled for the event?

- What could go wrong?

- Do you have enough food?

- What did you learn from the last one?

- What could be done better?

CAPTURE THE PROCESS!

Make sure you capture the process every step of the way. When you are done, file it and start building your marketing operations manual. Refer to each plan, capture them all but use the previous plans to improve each and every plan.

Here is an example of what I use for tracking and planning for a marketing campaign.

MARKETING CALENDAR
Worksheet

EVENT NAME:	ROCK, PAPER, SCISSORS

DESCRIPTION:
Play Rock, Paper, Scissors Tuesday Feb 3rd. with the cashier to get 1/2 off your bill at check out.

COST	
BUDGET	$700
ACTUAL	$640
DIFFERENCE	$60

Material Needed:	Quantity
3'x5' posters and celiing hangers.	6
Check Out Post cards: 50	40

TASKS	DATE	Assigned to:
Staff Meeting	Dec. 30	Rob
Post on Face Book	Jan. 1	Vince
Post on Website	Jan. 1	Vince
Hang Posters	Jan. 1	Rob
Fill guest check with Cards	Jan. 1	Stacey

METRICS	
Slowest Day of the Week	Tuesday
Avg. Guest Count	120
Historical PPA	$15.58
Historical Avg. Sales	$1,869.60

RESULTS	
Actual Guest Count	223
% of wins	67%
Per Person Ticket Avg.	$16.52
Total Sales before comps.	$3,683.96
Total Sales Actual	$2,468.25
Difference	-$1,215.71
Food Cost	28%
Total Cost of Food	-$340.40
Total Cost of Printed Mate	-$270
Total Cost of Promotion	-$610.40

ROI	
Previous Sales	$1,869.60
Event Sales	$3,683.96
Cost	-$610.40
Total ROI in + Sales	$1,203.96

LAUNCH IT

Build up the preshow. Make sure to announce that it is coming. Post it all over the restaurant. Promote it with staff and customers. Promote it on Facebook. Tell everyone you know. The movie is usually good but the preview makes it sell!

TRACK IT!

Each event you do should be measureable. Each gift card, ball, Facebook promotion, Password, etc. should have a unique way of tracking it. That is why you only do 3 at a time. Each time one comes in, record it.

Write the marketing campaign name on top of comp tickets and add them up at the end of the day check out.

- Keep a log.

Have multiple keys in your POS that track multiple different comp types. Have a Facebook button, a Yelp button, a loyalty button, etc. Run a p-mix report at the end of the week or month to track the number of times the button was used. Almost all POS system can track it this way.

RECORD IT!
- Record the number of returns you had.
- Record the amount spent.
- Record the cost of the per-person spend.
- Record the profit made.
- Capture the process and file it.

RINSE, WASH AND REPEAT!

Once you record multiple processes go back through and pull out your most successful ones. Dump or tweak the losers and rework, redo and reengineer your winners.

THE PROCESS

This may be the most valuable part of the book and this part can be applied to everything you want in life.

1.) Start with the end in mind.

2.) Draw an actual map with the beginning at one end and the end on the other side, like a pirate map.

3.) Go to the end and above it, write the goal you are trying to accomplish.

4.) Back up one step along your map and write what would have to happen right before that result.

5.) Then go back another step and write the result that would have to happen right before that outcome.

6.) Repeat this process all the way back to the beginning.

7.) Now read your map forward, rearrange, add missing steps and poof, you have a process map!

8.) Once the map is done, follow it step by step. Keep improving it along the way.

You have just done your first process map. Capture this and follow the process every time. For everything you ever need… follow this process. Google "Process Maps" or YouTube "Process Map" to see how this is done, especially if you are a more visual person.

Capture the process, print it, punch it with a three hole punch and put it in a book and build a systems manual for the entire restaurant or business. By the time you are done with everything in your business you will also have a step by step plan to delegate to an employee, manager, partner, etc. You now have the knowledge to "make it print'!

SEGMENT MARKETING

"We cannot solve our problems with the same thinking we used when creating them."
~ Albert Einstein

Segment Marketing is the targeted approach to your business in a very specific way. Most concepts have 9 segments or sales paths. Target marketing will help you develop the segment that needs the most improvement or at least avoid marketing to the one that needs it the least. I will cover the 9 segments but first I want you to imagine someone coming up to you offering to make the busiest part of your week even busier… with a proven marketing concept. Imagine I could show you a way to make your waiting list longer on Friday and Saturday. Sound good? Of course it doesn't. There is no really separation value when it comes to "being the weeds". I have never heard someone say we were only a little in the weeds. The truth is, Friday and Saturday are usually taken care of, unless you are a breakfast concept in which case Saturday and Sunday are usually taken care of. Either way, making your busiest segment busier would probably only hurt things. Thus, I ask you to consider your "Segment Marketing" strategy. Here is a breakdown on the 9 segments and some ideas on how to attack them separately and effectively.

1.) In Service Morning
2.) In Service Evening
3.) In Service Special Event
4.) Delivery Business Morning

5.) Delivery Business Evening
6.) Catering Morning
7.) Catering Evening
8.) Retail In Service
9.) Retail Out Service
  * Charity (This can be considered a segment)

Here is the breakdown and definition of these services along with a few quick ideas on how to market them.

IN SERVICE MORNING

This is typically lunch business done inside the restaurant. Majority of the Bonus Ideas in the next chapter fit this type of marketing, however, within this segment you are likely still not looking to promote business during your peak times. That is why it is critical to think about your offering. When running a promotion or event gear them towards not peak times and days. For example, if you were to do a face book add with a riddle or a guessing game that is going to give away lunch for two or a certain value, make the card only usable during lunch Sunday thru Thursday for example. *(If you are a breakfast and lunch concept than this would be breakfast and "In Service Evening" would be lunch)*

IN SERVICE EVENING

This is typically dinner business done inside the restaurant. Majority of the Bonus Ideas in the next chapter will also fit this type of marketing, however, within this segment you are likely still not looking to promote business during your peak times either. Again, that is why it is critical to think about your offering. When running a promotion or event, gear them towards non-peak times and days as well. For example, if you were to do a Facebook ad for a picture contest that is going to give away a wine dinner for two, make the redemption or event usable or scheduled during dinner Sunday thru Wednesday for example. *(If you are a breakfast and lunch concept than this would be lunch service)*

IN SERVICE SPECIAL EVENT

This area is one that is often missed or over looked. Special Events can be a marketing events specific to the restaurant like an Anniversary Party, holding a Red Carpet Event for an Oscar's Party, Having a "Special Guest" in to cook or a "Book Signing", a "Concert Series" etc. But it can also be a restaurant "Buy Out", a private party (either in a PDR or a portioned part of the restaurant), breakfast with Santa Claus, the Easter Bunny or even a principal on a back to school night. There are all sorts of tandem marketing approaches and segmented promotional events to consider in this category but having a protocol and a list of services, menus and cost attached to traditional special events should be considered so that the marketing efforts and impact will be promotable.

NOTE: Always remember when doing any segmented marketing campaign to keep your audience in mind. Also remember your audience is not the entire world, state, city or even a district. Keep your efforts local and *specific. All marketing segments need to appeal to a specific type of audience(s). You would not likely target the exact same crowd for a breakfast with Santa as you would a Oscar's Party. That being said, think about segments of your current audience that might compliment or be a target rich environment for an event that would appeal to them. The people that do "Breakfast with Santa Claus" would be an ideal audience for an Easter Egg hunt or "Breakfast with the Easter Bunny" Think about your audience whenever thinking up the event. Bounce the target audience question off of your staff and advisory board to see who the collective would consider your audience and then build a plan to get your messaging front of them. Pay special attention in the bonus section to the Facebook Marketing portion that talks about "Targeted Selection". All of the types of people and their likes and interests have been boiled down and stratified by Face Book and for as little as $5 a day you can send an add to a number of prequalified targets for any specific type of event... but more on that later*

Additionally: *If any of the ideas mentioned above sound good, make sure you under sell and over deliver the event. Often times it done in reverse order. Your cousin Sal should not be the drunk Easter Bunny in a bad rental costume with stains and the look that will give children nightmares. Hire a service and add an Easter egg hunt brunch to the docket. Set up a crafts table for doing eggs (you can boil the eggs and sell them as an additional profit center but make sure you hire of find someone with a strong background in the activities that knows how to manage the station and the kids, boast the fact that it will give the parents a little break if they like. Have a professional photographer and an Easter backdrop set up to do pictures with an opportunity to buy* *the picture framed or for sale for download on your website or theirs. (Think Sea World or any other amusement park that gets you coming and going). At a minimum give the pictures away for free on a share upload site and get permission to post them on your Face Book page too, to both promote the restaurant and to have imagery for the follow years ad campaign.*

For an event like the Oscars Party, rent a red carpet and hire a paparazzi for the event. Have prizes build around preselecting winners and build a lot of hype and live awards when the winner is picked. "Use an odds maker to weigh the value of the prize relative to the winner – speaking from experience". Hire a limo and stage it out front for a few hours before you open. Have a rotating spotlight swirling "Vegas Style" at the front entrance. Hire a valet service, etc. etc.

As with any of these ideas, if you want them to have a large impact you have to plan them well in advance, get the world excited and a buzz about them. Offer free tickets preceding the event (tied to something else) to build hype and appeal. These are a great thing to give to Radio Stations as prizes – they love giving away prizes and that gets you free mention. Also so an ROI calculator on the event. Budget the total cost for the event and then forecast the average spent you think people will have. Divide that number by your total and that should give you a good idea of head count in order for a break even. If the number seems reasonable, move forward, if not, modify.

DELIVERY BUSINESS MORNING

People like to eat in, whether it is at home or at a hotel, smart business are jumping all over this. Having a well-planned, executable process for delivery business is imperative. The average home has often been relegated to Italian, Pizza and Asian fare when it comes to home delivery. Even worse, the average hotel guest (myself included) has been relegated to the shitty "room service gouging" that most hotels call in-room dining. [If you are a hotelier know this, either undercharge and under deliver or overcharge and over deliver but the overcharging under delivering is on the precipice of giving way in the very near future]

In recent years a number of consolidation type, third party, delivery companies have popped up to ease this bourdon on the operator and in some cases this can create a new and valuable revenue stream otherwise not tapped into.

BUYER BEWARE: make sure if you are going to go with a third party that you understand how they operate. I have seen these third parties copy a menu and inflate the prices… that may work for you or it may leave a bad taste of over inflated pricing in your customer's mouth. Either way, look into it and see if there are options for you or investigate the option of building and in many cases improving your delivery model. For the best in the business this is a critical revenue center and one most could not live without now that they have tasted success in this arena and understood the reach and impact it has on your audience.

DELIVERY BUSINESS EVENING

This is another segment that has not been given good attention by many restaurants. Again, consider you offering and your packaging and what will travel well. You may need to have a limited delivery menu (with exceptions and disclaimers added when a guests asks for something specific they have had in house before). Then build a plan around your messaging, branding, and presentation of this material. Apply the same set of rules and considerations as mentioned above for building this program intelligently. Look at your competition and even the delivery business you, your friends and your family swear by at their house and use that as an outline to what you will and won't do in your program. In addition decide who your audience is and find a way to reach them. I am not a huge fan of direct mailers but in this case and with some impactful marketing materials I will buy address from the USPS for targeted zip codes and even more targeted people within those zip codes. For example, we use to buy a list of all new occupants in the surrounding zip codes of our restaurant so that we could do a little triple duty.

#1. We would welcome them to the neighborhood and introduce ourselves on the cover of our delivery menu with a map on how to get there.

#2. We would put a special offer for dining in with us since they were new to the neighborhood (like a free bottle of wine or 1 entrée on us).

#3. And of course that was all built into our delivery menu on one foldout page within the menu itself.

We placed the coupon in the menu to track the return rate on the marketing idea. We would track the zip codes that we would deliver to so that we could also track the impact of that part of the marketing agenda. In a zip code that returned high for us we would retarget that zip for other offers and for zips that didn't return so well for us we would put some room in between the cycles or try a different approach.

One of my favorite direct mail ad campaigns for delivery was simply putting a high gloss photo of delicious looking chicken soup on a post card and sending out the post card complete with an easy but delicious home recipe on the back. In addition to the recipe it had our website and a cute little phrase like…

"It's too cold to go outside!
Here's a favorite recipe of ours to keep you warm".
Don't feel like cooking, we have free delivery."
ourwebsite@us.com

CATERING MORNING

Definition: Out service business is single order business even if multiple people order. It is off menu and just like eating out but packed to go. Catering is different. Specifically catering is from a separate grouped style menu. One with options for scalability, size, and often it has a perceived value as a menu with a bundled discount price and packages. Catering can exist both in "drop off" form and "full service". While drop off is understood, full service means you bring the whole set up to the facility complete with small wares, warmers, serving utensils, chaffing dishes and even staff. You do not have to offer both but be clear what it is you offer. (Remember, you do not have to be everything to everyone!)

This is a segment often under marketed and certainly one that is under branded and under packaged. There are a number of vehicles to help you get the word out but you will need to make sure the Morning Catering marketing campaign is not just lumped in to your overall marketing efforts. Segment marketing is so effective because it addresses each particular part of your business as a specifically market segment. That is not to say that you can use the same template, theme and even delivery model but if you have done majority of the work think of how much more impactful it would be to change the segment name instead of adding the little asterisk at the bottom of the page or table tent that says **"We offer catering too!"**

I like to build a display of packing and Menuing in front of the store (where applicable), on the website, in the hall way, on Facebook, etc. Pay the little extra to have some nice images taken. Pay careful attention to how the product is packaged. One concept I have worked with does a flat bottom logo'ed box (like a soda can cardboard flat with their logo on it) and they wrap the food in a clear cellophane bag and tie the top with a ribbon that is the same as their brand color. This looks really elegant, unique and upscale and more importantly it is "Remarkable". People oh and awe when they see this packaging and they are soon not to forget. Perfect seed to plant when looking at getting repeat orders in the morning catering segment.

CATERING EVENING

This concept doesn't differ too much from Morning

Catering but there are some considerations. The packaging, marketing and even the menu and branding should again be different even if they are similar. You are marketing to a different audience all together. Remember earlier in the book when we talked about how market shift happens in any demographic. During the day you have business people and in the evening it may be residential or vice versa. Either way, the argument to combine the packaging for "cross marketing" doesn't really resonate unless you are a single menu concept like a Chipotle or a similar type of concept that serves the same menu all day. In that case, compound your efforts all day.

RETAIL IN SERVICE

This is my favorite, most overlooked category of all and huge profit center for those who are savvy enough to pay attention.

Consider your concept and what makes you different, better, special and most importantly... destination driven. Maybe you have a secret sauce, a unique recipe or spice, a marketable, unique or funny brand... have no shame, sell it!

It has been argued (unsuccessfully) by a few operators that they do not want to sell the secret spice or sauce or whatever because if they do then people won't need to come back. They can replicate the experience at home for a fraction of the price and instead of $40 in a ticket price they only get $5 in the secret ingredient sale. Read that back again if you agreed! Really? If you are a one trick pony only capturing people with one great recipe you had better read this book 10 times!

Sell your unique stuff! Don't be afraid to sell whole brined or even roasted turkey's for the holiday. Feel free to feature a whole prime rib for Christmas. Off to sell dessert or have a dessert case in a retail venue.

Do you have cool cooking tools? Look at the success of William and Sonoma or Sur la Table. They are killing it! Practically everyone is getting into this area in the big retailers and certainly you probably buy these products wholesale. Look at the difference in price you pay for a zester or a Teflon egg pan and then look at the what the consumer retail price is. Notice that gap? That means revenue to you. Cool glass ware, shakers, strainers, spill mats, nice KNIVES! Do you have a favorite widget people should know about? Do you smoke meats in your restaurant? Can you bundle 5 or 6 pieces of the wood in your plastic wrap and sell it for people to take home?

Merchandising – This is the art of the display. If you have ever walked into any nice boutique store you will notice the attention they pay to limiting the number of items on the shelves, the room they put between displays. The lighting, the cabinetry, etc. All of this precision crafting and eye appeal is part of a concept called merchandising. Take a look at an Apple store or a Whole Foods and pay close attention to how they display things. They are not cluttered and messy but rather elegant and sexy. Just like the craft applied to plate presentation, so to is retailing and it is called Merchandising. The product can be displayed in a based or wine box or bundled in a display. Shirts, hats, cups, spices, sauces... they can all flow together like a symphony to cleat elegant eye appeal. Consider this idea and look at all of the opportunity missed. Like most sales opportunities I like to place these things in areas where the people congregate or where lines are formed. Another great example is Starbucks. Do you think they sell some retail? Gift cards alone make up double digit store sales for this company…hmmm!

A RANDOM NOTE: My children love Chick-fil-A. I took them to one a few weeks back on a road trip and I noticed even Chick-fil-A has made a modest stab at retailing product. They now sell their signature dressing, honey mustard sauce and a few other items in nice retail packed containers at the front counter.

RETAIL OUT SERVICE

Now imagine you do have an in-store retail and merchandising strategy. Do you think it should end there? The answer, of course, is a resounding no!

If you have it in your restaurant you should feature it on line. Many people will go to your website either before or after visiting you live and in person. People from out of town will visit you, people who know people who love you will go to your online store. There is a very compelling reason to invest in an internet storefront on your website. The cost is modest. Setting up a retail pay-pal account is simple (Google it). The one tricky piece can be fulfillment.

I understand the challenge fulfillment can create but there is a solution. I use a print on demand company called **Galloree.com**
and they are amazing. You send in your art work (hi-res) and you can design all of your own stuff. I did all of my T-shirts, cups, mugs, stickers, bags, water bottles, etc. right on

their site. It is as simple as it can be.

Here is the reason to consider an on demand partner for retailing.

1.) You do not have to hold inventory on hand.
2.) You do not have to ship the product.
3.) You do not have to hope it all sells.

They do the shipping. You post the item on your page and when the customer clicks to order the item the page order goes to the site. You do not make as much money but where else can you make money never touching a product, paying in advance, etc.?

As for things that cannot be done through an on demand company like sauces, pots, pans, glassware, etc. I would still feature them on your website but I would note that those are available in store only. Companies like Target, Best Buy and Williams and Sonoma have already conditioned the market to this as a common practice.

Lastly, consider the value of your purchasing dynamic, where most people do not have an EIN nor do they purchase wholesale, think of the offering you could scale down to people through things and items you already buy. Is there a demand? I would ask myself that question and see what I could do to be a reasonably profitable middle man to bridge that gap!

SUMMARY: In rephrasing the message I have highlighted over and over in this book and boiling it down for a clean take away, you need to look at your business as a food service hub with multiple different businesses or departments operating under one roof. Of all of the segments listed above, consider you efforts individually and have a committee of people from your team of marketing and sales people dedicated to each: the presentation, packaging, sales agenda and training, the marketing materials, measuring and ROI and the demographics or audiences each effort will reach.

If you treat your business this way (even if it is the same team doing all of the work but approaching it by segment) you will start to understand the value of the "Profit Center" and the best practices that the elite in this business use and what they credit as a process that puts and keeps them on top. That is segmentation!

BONUS IDEAS

"When a gift is deserved, it is not a gift but a payment."
~ Gene Wolfe

You deserve this bonus gift because you made it this far. Because you have read this book I believe you are going to take action. As you have noticed, the ideas are worthless without the process and implementation. As most good ideas are. They end up in a journal, typed in a computer or in the recesses of our minds. There is nothing worse to me than having an idea and doing nothing with it. It is with this, that I shall start a chaotic list of crazy ideas I have seen and done that you can use to fill up your marketing calendar.

STICK IT!

Here is an amazing idea from one of my favorite clients ever, the Jelly Café in Denver! Their sticker is full color hot pink, just like their logo.

Start an in-store and a Facebook campaign for a

"FREE LUNCH" @ your restaurant.

On Facebook:

Header: FREE LUNCH! (Include image of the sticker on the post – best if done literally like taking a picture of your sticker on the bumper of a car or your forehead or on a baby…something like that)

<u>Caption:</u> **Get your at the "Whatever Street" location and show us where you "stick it".**
Simply put your sticker anywhere you like and upload a picture of it on our Facebook Page.

We will pick a winner every day for the month of "Your slowest month" to win a free lunch (Valued at $10, lunch only).

<u>***Winners will be announced each day at 9:00 am**</u>

STAFF: Have the staff promote the very same idea in the store when they drop off the guest check.
Have them include 4 stickers with each guest check (Jelly printed their rules on the back of the stickers.)

BENEFIT – People must go to your FB page see who won. This will require them to like your page and build a larger fan base.

TRACKING – This is 100% trackable and creates direct customer connection/rapport.

COST: PSPrinting.com has a 60% off deals all the time. Regular cost of 1000 stickers is $180 before discount. Facebook Labor for 1 month ($300). Cost of 30 $10 meals

@ 33% cost of goods = $100

Total Cost $580

ROI – The average table size in your restaurant is likely 2.7 people if you are like most US concepts. I am sure your average guest spend is close to the industry average of $13.

The ROI calculator would say this
>   **2.7 guests per table**
>   **$13 per person spend**
>   **30 days (30 winners)**

= $1,530 revenue

= $580 spend

= $950 ROI

Or nearly $3 earned on $1 spent (this is an outrageous return for any marketing effort)

Measure the impact!

Count total number of FB fans before the event starts and count the total number of fans at the end (or page likes). The difference is a realistic measurable impact of how many people this reached.

Add up total number of submissions per day for the entire month. That is the level 1 reach plus the level two reach of all the friends of those that posted and shared (exponential attention).

*ADDED BONUS – Here is a fun multiplier for additional return. Reply individually to all people who submitted an FB post and let them know they didn't win but you wanted to give them a runner up reward just for trying. Let them know that if they send you their email you will send them a $5 gift card as a thank you to them. Capture the email as an "opt in" and add them to your data base for continued

marketing.
LUNCH IS ON US (Gift Cards)

FEET ON THE STREET CAMPAIGN

Have a few local business merchants you know, couriers, delivery companies and/or trusted business customers that patronize your restaurant (real-estate people, car salesmen, brokers, bankers, etc.). Ask them to participate in this effort. Upon agreement, give each of them a complimentary card for themselves for helping out (or buy them lunch) and extend a number of cards to each of the people that you enlist to help with this effort. We also encourage the owners to visit local business to do a meet and greet, introduction and pass out cards as well.

The pitch to those handing out the cards. "Hey so & so, I am neighbors with "Your Restaurant Name" on "Whatever Street" and I agreed to hand out these gifts cards for them to help promote their new lunch menu. I got to try a few of their new items and they are amazing. Here's a $10 gift card. If you get a minute go see them for lunch!"

or

Pitch from your customer who is a business professional: It was a pleasure doing business with you here at the "bank, car lot, etc.", here are a couple gift card for "Your Restaurant's Name" down the street. Go enjoy lunch on me!

Pitch from the local Car Dealer: If you folks want to take this car on a test drive and grab some lunch to talk it over, here is a gift card to "Your Restaurant's Name", right down the street. Have a bite on me while you guys think it over."

And so on and so forth…

The pitch from the owners/managers of your restaurant while out on the street: Hi, I'm so & so from "Your Restaurant's Name" and I wanted to come by an introduce myself as your neighbor. Have you been to "Your Restaurant's Name"? Great, well we wanted to go around to our neighbors and hand out some free gift cards so that you can come in and try our new lunch menu. No strings attached. This is 10 free dollars worth of anything on our menu, Monday – Thursday at lunch time. Ask for me when you come in so can hi to you!

- I would run this promo for two months.

BENEFIT – Each card is sequenced with numbers so you can measure the return and from which group of people they were distributed. Keep a log of the cards before handing them out.

TRACKING – This is 100% trackable and creates direct

customer connection/rapport in your business community.
COST: CardPrinting.us will do 500 full color gift cards
(with magnetic strip) for around $.67 per card. For a total
of $351 including freight (feel free to use your own card
company just make sure they are sequenced for measuring)
Labor is free plus the cost of the card and the cost of
goods for the cards you give to the people who will
distribute for you.

This campaign usually sees about a 75% return rate on
cards distributed. Make sure to have a **"valid until date"**
on the card as a **"call to action"**.

TOTAL COST
$351 for cards
+ $1250 (375 $10 gift cards at 33% COGs) = **$1601**
ROI – The average table size in your restaurant is
likely **2.7 people** if you are like most breakfast
concepts. I am sure you average guest spend is **$13**

The ROI calculator would say this
   2.7 guest per table
   $13 per guest
   ***375 cards (75% expected return rate)**
= **$13,163 revenue**
= **$1601 spend**
= **$11,562 ROI**

Nearly $10 made on $1 spend (this is an outrageous
return for any marketing effort as well)

Measure the impact
Keep track of the sequence of cards and who you gave
them to. Record where the cards came back from.
Measure the date of delivery and the days of return to see

how soon (how effective) this marketing effort was in your area.

The people and the placed with the highest rate of return become the best places to target in your next campaign.

Following the last two ideas formatting, here are some additional ideas for you to consider or modify.

THE PHOTO BOOTH

Isolate a section in your restaurant to make a photo backdrop. Make it themed with your logo above where the average head height of the photo area. Include a wall with hooks that hold novelty props like eye glasses, moustaches, huge loafs of bread, giant wine glasses, funny hats, beards, props, etc.

Try to make the props match your theme and post a sign letting people know to post the image to your FB page. Have the QR code or website location of your FB page printed somewhere as well. Compound the idea with a **"wall of fame"** in that is framed from your best and most creative or funny photos from previous guests. This will create a concept called "social proof" by where if people see that others have done it they will be more inclined to do it too. Most people have phones and can take the photos but I have had clients even put up a mounted digital camera with a shutter button.

In addition to the idea of the photo booth, consider putting it in a high traffic area. I like to put it by the front door or the bathroom. That way when there is a line it distracts the guest form any inconvenience and instead promotes a fun and playful environment... all of which are great for any brand!

POSITIVE PICKETING

Have your employees stand outside with picket signs that advertise a new menu, a band playing tonight, an awesome happy hour. Sure it's crazy but it will get you attention and new customers too.

STUDIO 54 IT!

Create the false line. Hire people to stand in line outside of your business just to make it look busy. Research the studio 54 story if you are unfamiliar with it.

CREATE A BAD ASS MENU

This is your number one marketing vehicle. Make sure it is unique and in line with your concept. Make sure it screams your brands identity when people see it. Look for my next book coming soon about Menu Engineering and the art and science of aesthetics.

CO-SPONSOR A VACATION

Look for other likeminded industries to help sponsor a raffle vacation package. Check out some of the ideas on line and make them fit what you do.

CLOSE FOR A WEEK TO EDUCATE YOUR STAFF

There is an amazing concept in Denver, Colorado called the Barolo Grill. They are by far the best Northern Italian Restaurant concept in the state. Every year, they close for a month and take their entire staff to Italy. The front of the house tours vineyards and meets the growers, participates in new tastings and they pick the wines for the next seasons menu. The back of the house guys go stage (work for free in exchange for the wisdom) at multiple restaurants in the region and learn new techniques and find inspiration for next season's menu.

NOTE: I would be willing to bet, if you are ever in Denver you will eat there! Ask for Chef Daryl and tell him Ron Bryant sent you and likely you will get a little extra special treatment!

For more great ideas on staff training read the book from Phoebe Damrosch called "Service Included" or "The Renegade Server" from Tim Kirkland.

A PROMOTION AROUND A RIDDLE

A kid who went through my "Epic Service" training took an idea I had given him about doing a riddle to build regular guests. The idea was pretty simple. When customers came in, he would ask them is they liked riddles. If they said no, it's not a big deal if they say yes; he would ask if they would like to play? He explained his rules. He gives them the riddle and lets them know that they can guess every time he comes to the table. If they solve the riddle before the end of the meal, he will buy them an after dinner drink or dessert. This creates what I like to call "dinner and a show". This idea could work in many different ways.

SPECIAL CALENDAR DAY

Check out the **daysoftheyear.com** website. There is pretty much a holiday or national day of something every day of the year. Today for example is "Chocolate Covered Anything Day". Do you see how you could look at this calendar and build some marketing hype around it one way or another?

TV PREMIER/AWARDS SHOW PARTY

Find out who your audience is and do a season premier or an awards show viewing party based around what they watch on TV. Create food and drink specials, have a contest for best dressed, worst dressed, have a red carpet, take pictures and post them around the restaurant or on Facebook and/or your website, etc. I have actually done events like this that we bring in local celebrity, have gambling pools and games for picking the winners, hire a film crew, roll out a red carpet, hire paparazzi, etc. The idea pays off in food, drink, word of mouth and other prizes.

THE GLASS IS HALF FULL

A tremendous little marketing piece we did to build our lunch business happened when we started offering a half glass of beer or wine at lunch. The response was amazing. People can really rationalize not breaking the rules when it is only half of a rule. It was more like a tasting than having a drink. Just a little something to compliment the food. As least that's what we told them. And… apparently they listened.

THANK YOU CARD

This is one of my personal favorites. Particularly because this happened to me as a customer as opposed to it being one of my own ideas. Trust me; it later became one of my ideas.

The story goes something like this. It was a week before my wife's birthday and I decided to make a "reso" at a great restaurant I had been dying to try. I called the restaurant and the conversation went something like this.

TRUE STORY

Thanks for calling Panzano, this is Becky.

Me: Hi Becky, I would like to make a reservation for next Friday if I could.

Becky: Absolutely sir. What time did you want to join us?

Me: I was hoping you might have something around 7:00.

Becky: We sure do. Is that the time that would work best for you?

Me: Uh… actually, do you have anything at 6:30?

Becky: We do. Can I get your name?

Me: Yes, It's Ron Bryant

Becky: *Thank you Mr. Bryant! How many people will be in your party?*
Me: *Two of us.*

Becky: *Wonderful, thank you Mr. Bryant. Do you have additional plans and are you celebrating anything special next Friday?*

Me: *Yes, we will be going to a show at 9:30 and we are celebrating my wife's birthday.*

Becky: *How wonderful, what is your wife's name?*

Me: *Jennifer.*

Becky: *Okay Mr. Bryant, we look forward to having you and Jennifer in next Friday at 6:30. I will get you a great table and I will also let your server know you have a time constraint. It shouldn't be a problem getting you out by 9:30 but I will make her aware. Lastly, Mr. Bryant, if I could get your phone number, we like to make a phone call the day before as reminder just in case your plans have changed.*

Me: *Okay. Then I gave her my phone number.*

It was a very professional and pleasant experience and my expectation was already high because of such a thoughtful and personal exchange but that isn't even the best part.

When we arrived that Friday night, we were greeted as if they knew exactly who we were. Becky greeted us and wished my wife a happy birthday and led us to a beautiful, romantic table. When we got to the table, there was an envelope on the table.

My wife looked at me with doe eyes like I had arranged the whole thing and I had some special pull because, of course, I am the "restaurant guy." Not even a little bit. I was just as curious about the envelope with my wife's name on it as she was. When she opened it, there was a card with a classically designed cover where upon opening it, a simple little message read **"Thanks for spending your special day with us."**

Then in pen it read, "Happy Birthday". And the card was signed by what appeared to be every single member of the staff in black and/or blue ink.

The chef also sent out a complimentary tasting plate that was not part of every table's experience. Pretty bad ass huh?

So, I am not sure where the lines of marketing get blurred with amazing service but I tell this story to anyone who will listen so I would deem this a "Remarkable Marketing" idea.

Even though my restaurant at the time didn't take reservations, we still found a way to incorporate this idea. I have always hated the idea of the singing server conga line and I wasn't crazy about giving away a free desert and embarrassing people. This was what I would call an elegant solution.

The card idea was a lot more personal than a dessert (don't do what everyone else does). The card also cost us about $.35 in bulk vs. the average dessert at my place which cost us about $1.60. Every time we had a staff meeting I would have the entire team sign about 100 cards and boy did we use them. This little idea also had a surprise little outcome. We decided we would not only card everyone that ordered an alcoholic beverage; (regardless of their age) we would really look at the birth date not just the year.

> **NOTE:** *If people get irritated when being carded, studies have found that when you actually give it back, thanking them personally by name, the edge goes away and out comes a smile.*

My staff was crazy about the idea because it endeared the customer to that server and they usually made a better tip. We would then give the customer who had a birthday yesterday, today or tomorrow a sealed envelope to the same effect (*as the story above) when we dropped the bill. Specifically placing the card in front of the birthday boy or girl (or the anniversary person, if we caught that info). The impact was amazing, and it really ensured everyone was carded… nice added bonus.

> **FACT**(ish): *I have heard, but have never substantiated, that over 80% of the population celebrates their birthday out at a restaurant.*

INTENTIONALLY MESSED UP SIGNS

We would intentionally hang banners upside down when promoting something on the outside of the restaurant. The banner was a simple and impactful offer with only a few words. The idea came to me when I read a research study that showed how the human brain could read thing upside down almost as fast they could read something upside right. It was silly but it fit our personality and really got people's attention.

THE OL' FAKE PARKING TICKET

Now this one pushed the boundaries but at Hella Burger we could pull off anything edgy because that is who we were, top to bottom!

I found a place on line that sold fake parking ticket envelopes. (Get them at **funslurp.com**)

During the months of April we decided to prank some new, would be, customers. We called this one "April Fools Marketing"

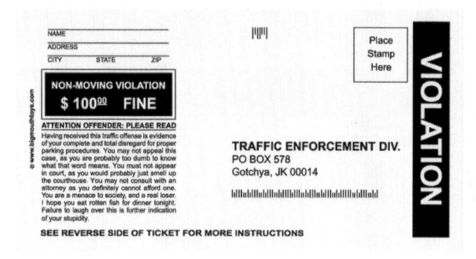

We would fill these fake parking tickets with a funny ticket. Inside it would say, Warning! When parking in this parking lot you need to visit Hella Burger! In fact, here's $10 bucks (gift card) on us. Come try a damn good burger next time you are here. What the hell, if people don't have a sense of humor they weren't our type of customer anyway. It actually created a ton of funny feedback on viral marketing and tons of word of mouth for us.

Crazy? Sure, but you don't get results from being average or just like everyone else.

SELL A PERSONAL CHEF PACKAGE

We use to advertise having our chef come into your home for a party as small as 6 up to 100. Starting at $20 per person. We would do the cooking, consult on free menu and bring all of the food. You could really get crazy with this one. We had great success with it but we didn't ride it for all that it was worth.

GET STUCK

We loved the bumper sticker idea. I grew up in Montana and every cowboy I knew had some obscure funny named bar bumper sticker on their car. When we developed our brand and logo for Hella Burger we printed stickers. Not bumper stickers but those black and white oval stickers with the initials of the brand. We handed them out like crazy. We saw them on cars, windows, stop signs, etc. One day I was at a business meeting on the other side of town and when meeting my client at a Starbucks and I saw a kid rocking our sticker on his Apple Laptop. That was when I felt like I had really made it.

We use to also put a version of our stickers on our box lunches where we could write the name of the item in the box along with the person's name if we knew it.

EXCLUSIVE FUNNY T-SHIRTS

We had a list of special tongue in cheek tee-shirts made that we sold retail. Our chicken sandwich (ha, ha, I know) was actually a ground chicken burger made with herbs, achiote and brandy and we appropriately called it the "Drunk Chick". It did really well but the following came from the tee-shirt. The front had our logo and read… I ate a "drunk chick".

We also had shirts that had a logo with the words Devil's Advocate, Handsome Little Devil, I am the Drunk Chick! It created a sweet little cult following and again, it was genuinely representative of us and our brand. We had many more but these were some of my favorite.

VOTING SIGNS IN THE YARD

You know those signs that you put in the yard when you believe so blindly in a candidate during election time? Yeah, me neither but I did see a great idea in this logic, it was just misapplied. The signs are actually called "Bandit Signs" and I have seen them for as little as $.99 on line. Whenever I work with a concept that has a home delivery business I always lead with this one. We basically ask every customer if they would like to receive $10 off their order tonight. If they were interested, we would tell them what we were up to. We have a tasteful and funny yard sign that has our name on it. It's a marketing sign similar to the kind you see in people's yards during election season. Our sign says...

When the neighbors would call and mention the sign, we would tell them that they could get $10 off too. All they had to do was put the same sign in their yard after we delivered their food.

I don't know how long these signs stayed in the yard but they were cheap, the customer got a deal and the neighbor became aware of a new delivery guy on the block. It created a lot of word of mouth in the neighborhood and around the water cooler.

Now go take one of these ideas or modify one and go make it print. If you really loved this, I will send you a Power Point presentation of many more crazy ideas you can use.

Want more? Got questions? Want updates or a little banter back and forth? Hit us up at...

BoBryant.com

Best of luck and I leave you with my favorite quote of all time. It came from a campaign launch that Apple did in 1997...

"Here's to the crazy ones. The misfits. The rebels. The troublemakers. The round pegs in the square holes. The ones who see things differently. They're not fond of rules. And they have no respect for the status quo. You can quote them, disagree with them, glorify or vilify them. About the only thing you can't do is ignore them. Because they change things. They push the human race forward. And while some may see them as the crazy ones, we see genius. Because the people who are crazy enough to think they can change the world, are the ones who do."

— Apple Inc.